A MIND OF ONE PIECE

A MIND OF ONE PIECE

Brandeis and American Reform

by Melvin I. Urofsky

CHARLES SCRIBNER'S SONS/New York

Printed in the United States of America
Library of Congress Catalog Card Number 74-143945
SBN 684-12368-1

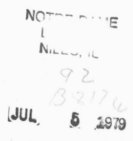

With love and appreciation,
to my parents and my wife's parents

CONTENTS

PREFACE

It is a truism that we live in an age of bigness—big business, big government, big unions, big cities, and big problems. We have a gross national product approaching one trillion dollars, and enterprises involving millions of dollars are now considered moderate ventures. Statistics about American life all point up our gigantic size: we drive more cars, use more electricity, eat more food, generate more garbage, drink more liquor, make more money, and have more pollution than any other nation in the history of the world.

Why then a book about a man who considered bigness to be a curse, who fought all his life for smallness, for manageable units, for diversity that can only be found, as he put it, "on a wee scale"? What is there in the life of Louis Dembitz Brandeis that we, who are the children of Leviathan, should find so interesting? After all, he failed to halt the march toward consolidation and centralization, the big companies he opposed are now overshadowed themselves by gigantic corporations and conglomerates, and the federal government which he had hoped to restrict now affects every facet of its citizens' lives.

To ask these questions is in some measure to answer them. We have always been a nation that drives inexorably toward accomplishment on a grand scale while simultaneously yearning for an older, simpler, and supposedly less hectic style of life.

The bigger and more powerful we get, the less happy we seem with our size, the less able to control our power. Perhaps worst of all, we have failed to grow in moral stature to keep up with our material expansion. In a nation of wealth, there is far too much poverty; in a society committed to justice, there is too much prejudice and injustice; in times that call for reason, we have seen too much insanity.

A similar malaise of contradictions afflicted the progressives, who saw poverty in the midst of wealth, injustice and prejudice, and the growth of large blocs of power threatening democratic processes. To these problems Louis Brandeis addressed himself: he attempted to formulate new modes by which the old principles of liberty, justice, and democracy could be applied in a transitional society. He was unable to halt certain historic trends, but he was effective in dealing with many of the problems generated by those trends, in humanizing a growing governmental structure, in tempering big business by making it accountable to people, in insisting that the law serve public rather than private needs. He utilized the "system's" own rules and mores and forced it to come to grips with the problems of democracy, to respond to the will of the people. By working from within, he hoped to reform society, to uplift it, and to democratize it. Through all this work shone the clear light of his essential morality.

The theme of these essays is to show how seamless life and thought were in this man, how closely action and philosophy could be related in a single personality. As Paul Freund commented, Brandeis had "a mind of one piece." These essays, though, are not meant to be a biography; for that the reader is referred to Alpheus T. Mason, *Brandeis: A Free Man's Life* (New York, 1946). Newly opened manuscript resources as well as recent scholarship have provided us with material and insights that were unavailable twenty-five years ago. My purpose has been to supplement the standard biography with some thoughts on different aspects of Brandeis's life, and to illuminate the life of one of the important figures in the history of American reform.

Many of the ideas presented here grew out of my work on *The Letters of Louis D. Brandeis* (Albany, New York, 1971—), and one of my great debts is to my coeditor, David W. Levy of the University of Oklahoma, who carefully scrutinized the manuscript, and critically discussed these problems with me. The original impetus to write this book came from a conversation with Professor Jacob E. Cooke of Lehigh University and Thomas S. Davis III, then of Scribner's. Other people who undertook the chore of reading manuscript copy include my friends and colleagues Jerome Eckstein, Arthur Ekirch, and Helen Horowitz of the State University of New York at Albany. William Goldsmith and Hamilton Cravens also read the manuscript. Mary K. Tachau of the University of Louisville and Robert D. Cuff of York University both went well beyond the demands of friendship in their careful critiques of my work. Mr. and Mrs. Paul Raushenbush of Madison, Wisonsin, were as always generous in their help and understanding of matters pertaining to Brandeis. Norman Kotker of Scribner's guided the manuscript through the publishing maze. Their suggestions have made this a better book than it would otherwise have been; the flaws, however, devolve entirely on me. My wife, Susan, and our sons, Philip and Robert, demonstrated exemplary patience during the numerous times when I gave more attention to Clio than to them. The dedication is but a small acknowledgment of debts that can never be paid.

Melvin I. Urofsky

State University of New York at Albany

Chapter I

A REFORMER AND A TRADITION

His law partner once characterized Louis Brandeis as "more Brahmin than the Brahmins." If men are indeed shaped by their environment, as the social psychologists claim, then the influences that affected and molded Louis Dembitz Brandeis are to be found not only in the Kentucky of his boyhood, but even more in the transitional Boston of his young manhood and maturity. For no matter what his friends or foes may have claimed, Louis Brandeis was intellectually and emotionally a New Englander of the finest variety. Both his early acceptance into Boston's upper-class society and later that society's rejection of him resulted from his adoption of the older Brahmin belief in the need to reform society. To understand his later work, in both its strengths and shortcomings, we must begin by examining the milieu in which he developed.

Brandeis was born on November 13, 1856, in Louisville, a thriving commercial city on the Ohio River. The city sat in the midst of rich, well-tended lands, on a crossroads between the agrarian and industrial sections of the nation, and its merchants grew rich on trade. The city's prosperity had lured Adolph Brandeis there in 1851, and in partnership with Charles W. Crawford, he soon built up a highly successful grain and produce business.

Adolph and Frederika Brandeis moved easily in the limited but lively cultural and intellectual circles of Louisville. Well-read and articulate, they instilled in their four children a dedication to books and the arts, and a commitment to the rigorous examination of ideas. More importantly, they taught their offspring that the highest achievement in life was service to others. To her son, Frederika wrote: "I believe that only goodness and truth and conduct that is humane and self-sacrificing towards those who need us can bring God nearer to us, and that our errors can only be atoned for by our acting in a more kindly spirit. Love, virtue and truth are the foundations upon which the education of the child must be based. They endure forever." [1] This was the seed that would blossom so fully in Boston.

When Brandeis enrolled in the Harvard Law School in the fall of 1875, he entered a new world, both intellectually and socially. In 1880, Emerson, Longfellow, Bronson Alcott, Whittier, James R. Lowell, and the senior Holmes were all alive, carrying on a great literary tradition, while many of the leaders of the pre–Civil War reforms, such as Edward Everett Hale, Benjamin Sanborn, Thomas Wentworth Higginson, and Julia Ward Howe, still articulated the belief that for society to survive, it had to reform itself constantly.[2]

The living example of these men and women served as a magnet to attract a new generation of writers and reformers to Boston, people like John Boyle O'Reilly, Edwin Doak Mead and his wife, Lucia True Ames, Frank Parsons, Hamlin Garland, and Brandeis, who would carry on the great tradition. As Arthur Mann has noted, with the exception of Vida Scudder and Francis Greenwood Peabody, every important Boston reformer of the later nineteenth century came from outside the city, lured there by its heritage and excitement.[3]

At Cambridge, the life of the mind reigned supreme. In an essay describing the Law School, Brandeis later went out of his way to glorify the "intellectual self-reliance and spirit of investigation" which the new case-study method had stressed.[4] The value of exploring ideas for their own sake, which his parents had taught him, was now reinforced by the example set by the faculty, whom he admired greatly.[5] The classroom appealed to him so much that for several years he seriously contemplated giving up his private practice and becoming a legal scholar; only the excitement of courtroom battle prevented him from leaving the law office for the lecture hall.[6]

This life of the mind, however, was not limited to the corridors of the Law School's Dane Hall. Brandeis's brilliance, his charm, and his friendship with the socially prominent Samuel D. Warren soon made him welcome in the best of Boston's homes. There he was exposed to the full force of New England's intellectual, moral, and literary traditions, and there he met and was influenced by the last survivors of what Van Wyck Brooks has termed New England's "Flowering," the Transcendentalist illuminati.[7]

It would be incorrect to assert that Brandeis was immediately won over to the cause of genteel reform by his contacts with these people; he met nearly all of them, but they fascinated him primarily because of their intellectual qualities. It was not until close to the end of the century that he began devoting time to reform work on a substantial scale, but when he did begin, he immediately showed that in addition to his family's teachings, he had imbibed the basic assumptions of the earlier New England crusaders.

An essential component of that philosophy was a belief in the constant need to reform society, a need that in the past had led to a remarkable record of social progress. Massachusetts people had been in the forefront of the antislavery movement, as well as in the vanguards of feminism, prison and asylum reform, and expansion of the common school systems, to name but a few causes. Not only had the Bay State been among the first to be industrialized, it had also been among the first to respond legislatively to the social problems created by the factories. Massachusetts had pioneered in child labor laws (1836), instituted the first state factory inspection system (1866), and passed the first laws regulating working hours for women and children (1874). As Richard Abrams has shown, what progressives fought bitterly for in other states had long since been accepted as the norm in Massachusetts.[8]

This belief in the need to improve society and the substantive results of earlier reform efforts had created a unique tradition in the Bay State. First of all, reform had found a sympathetic resonance in the Puritan theology. Although man was born evil, he was capable of grace; more importantly, the earthly affairs of men were in their own hands, with a heavenly mandate to do good unto one another. From the seventeenth century on, it had been deemed the citizen's duty to work for the betterment of the commonweal. So accepted was the right of the private citizen to labor in the public interest that the General Court permitted nonmembers to introduce bills and petitions on the same basis as members.

Secondly, the leaders of past reformist causes had not been lower-class radicals, but middle- and upper-class professionals and businessmen, many of them Brahmins who took seriously their assumed stewardship of society. Through their activities, they placed a stamp of respectability upon efforts to change things as they were to things as they ought to be. In this milieu, therefore, to be a reformer was to be a conservative in the Burkean sense of the word, with a belief that the best way to preserve society was to build upon whatever was good and useful, and improve whatever was bad.

Brandeis always thought of himself as working within this tradition. To Henry Morgenthau, Sr., he declared that "true conservatism involves progress, and that unless our financial leaders are capable of progress, the institutions which they are trying to conserve will lose their foundation." [9] Even when attacking the vested interests of State Street, he mined a familiar vein in the Puritan distrust of the new finance capitalism; indeed, few states had such stringent laws as Massachusetts did to regulate corporate conduct and finance. A good part of Brandeis's attack on the Morgan-sponsored New Haven Railroad's attempt to monopolize New England's transportation system rested upon the charge that the road's managers were violating already existing Massachusetts law. [10]

Brandeis also drew heavily upon an older tradition which emphasized not only individual opportunity, but corresponding individual responsibility. The earlier proponents of reform had not assumed that the world would automatically get better. Rather, each person had to contribute to progress, and social evolution resulted from the collective, conscious efforts of individuals. The good society allowed each man to make the most of his own abilities, with the least possible interference from either the state or vested social, political, or economic interests. Whether he succeeded or not depended on his own talents; just as there should be no impediment to his strength, so there should be no artificial support for his weakness. In many ways, two centuries had done little to erase the Puritan equation of economic success with moral goodness; man must be free to test himself, Brandeis believed, but he also had to face the consequences of his failure.[11]

While striving for individual success, the good citizen—both alone and in groups—was under obligation to work to overcome artificial barriers to social improvement. Privately he should support charities for those unfortunates who fell by the wayside; publicly he had to keep an ever-vigilant eye upon the government and utilize it to eradicate false barriers to individual opportunity. These two functions—the drive toward success and civic responsibility—were the cornerstones of social progress. Fittingly, Brandeis thought highly of both Ralph Waldo Emerson and of Henry George, one the apostle of "Self-Reliance," the other the foe of artificial privilege.[12]

Brandeis capitalized on this tradition in the organization of public pressure groups. While not averse to working with select committees of leading citizens, he also wanted the backing of large groups in order to organize his battle around the theme of the public welfare vs. private interests.[13] The Savings Bank Insurance League and the Anti-Merger League had memberships numbering into the tens of thousands, yet their function was more than that of securing well-signed petitions; they carried the battle down to the level of each citizen. If the common man assumed even a small share of civic responsibility, the future progress of society would be assured; if he did not, all would be lost.[14] In many ways, this echoed the original Puritan view of a commonwealth of responsible citizens.

Not all of the Massachusetts tradition, however, was conducive to modern reform, and Brandeis shared its weaknesses. More than any other section of the country, New England has always displayed a certain insularity and standoffishness. While its citizens have frequently described this condition as "local pride" or "tradition," less sympathetic observers have termed it "parochialism." [15] This manifested itself in Brandeis's belief that, economically, New England was best able to look after its own interests, and that outside financial forces, especially those of New York, should be severely limited in the amount of business or the degree of control they could exercise in the Bay State.

This prejudice showed clearly in two of Brandeis's most important Massachusetts crusades, the fight to establish savings bank life insurance and the struggle against the New Haven Railroad's takeover of the Boston & Maine line. The Hughes investigation of insurance corruption in 1906 led a group of New England policyholders to retain Brandeis as counsel to protect their large interests.[16] Although he saw that the problem of insurance corruption extended beyond the protection of local policyholders, an important thrust of Brandeis's proposal aimed at keeping the business in New England under local control. "What we must hope for," he wrote in a typical letter, "is to develop home industry in insurance. Are we better for having been fleeced by New York Life, the Mutual, the Equitable and others than if we had had more Massachusetts Companies?" [17]

In the contest against the Morgan-dominated New Haven, Brandeis sounded this theme repeatedly. Time and again he cited an old state law forbidding out-of-state corporations from controlling local companies, and constantly urged lawmakers not to stray from this wise path of keeping Massachusetts in control of her own fate. Never once did he come to grips with the problems of modern finance or integrated transportation.[18] In his exposé of the money trust, this desire for local control shines through quite clearly, as does a wish to return to older days of simplistic, provincial isolation; here Brandeis spoke not only for himself but reflected the sentiments of many other

New Englanders.[19] Indeed, the entire fight against bigness has something of the parochial in it.

Brandeis's inclination to merge with the civic and intellectual traditions of Boston made it easier for him to join it socially. In an upper-class society which still paid homage to qualities of the mind, his brilliance had opened many doors. It is questionable, though, if he could have been so socially mobile a generation later; Brandeis came to Boston just before the mercantile élite froze into a hereditary caste. The wealth of the Bay State had been created in the eighteenth and early nineteenth centuries, first by oceanic commerce and then by industry. The traders and merchants of colonial and revolutionary Boston had laid the bases for many great fortunes, and, following the Puritan criteria, had assumed that commercial success earned them the leadership of the community. While some of them may have had aristocratic pretensions, for the most part society had accorded them deference in proportion to their real accomplishments.[20] In the decades prior to the Civil War, room at the top had been available to accommodate the new factory wealth.

After the Civil War, however, the old order had found itself boxed in from above and subject to increasing pressures from the bottom. Financial leadership of the country had moved to New York with the rise of the great banking houses there. To some extent, Boston's decline in this field had resulted from a continued Puritan disinclination to use money for speculative purposes. The Adams family's repugnance for the maneuverings of the Wall Street crowd reflected the older attitudes regarding the proper uses of money.[21] At the same time, a flood of immigrants had created new demands for mobility from below. By 1880, half of the Massachusetts population counted itself as either foreign born or the children of foreign-born parents; in the next three decades, this percentage shot up steeply, and many of the newcomers had settled in Boston.[22]

In what might be termed a failure of nerve, the old élite desperately attempted to consolidate their leadership by trans-

forming themselves into a hereditary caste. As Frederic C.
Jaher shows, the antebellum social flexibility gave way to the
rigidity of inherited status.[23] Seeking continuity over change,
the Brahmins erected the symbols of a hereditary society—old
schools, old clubs, English-sounding streets and residences, dou-
ble names, and so on. Moreover, as Arthur Mann notes, the
multiplication of trusts to protect family fortunes indicated
that Boston's élite had also lost its economic daring.[24] Although it was not immediately apparent, in grasping at the il-
lusion of permanent control, the Brahmins forfeited real
power.

The important point regarding Brandeis is that he had
come to Boston just in time. A good part of his later fame and
effectiveness would rest upon his entry into the right circles;
access might have been denied him had he arrived in Boston
only a few years later. A very eligible bachelor during the
1880s, he had been a frequent guest in the "best of homes," and
his success at the bar had won him membership in some of the
city's most exclusive social citadels—the Union, Exchange,
Union Boat, and Dedham Polo Clubs. Moreover, he had been
named to the committee to visit the Harvard Law School, a
prestige group comprised of those who met not only legal but
social criteria as well. When he had married Alice Goldmark in
March, 1890, the first person to call on the newly wed couple
had been Henry Lee Higginson's wife.[25] How importantly tim-
ing figured here can be seen by looking at men only a few years
junior to Brandeis. Elias M. Lowe and Howard Johnson, who
made their respective millions in theaters and restaurants, as
well as railroad magnates C. P. Clark, Onslow Stearns, and F.
L. Ames, were all barred from entry into the inner social circles.[26]

I am not suggesting that Brandeis would not have been a
successful lawyer had he been barred from Boston society; his
legal brilliance and keen sense of business would have brought
him clients in any event. But, he did not want to be "some-
body's lawyer," he wanted to be an independent attorney, and
that meant he had to stand as an equal to his clients. Social acceptance assured him of that position.

Brandeis could not avoid, however, the resentments generated by the new stratification. Some of the "pure-blooded" members of his club, already succumbing to caste-consciousness, resented his presence, and his daughters remember that although they were enrolled in the best private school in the city, the teachers always were asking which of the students came from the "old" families.[27] Even allowing for this, we should note the relative lack of anti-Semitism in Boston in the later nineteenth century. The torrents of hatred directed against Brandeis during the fight over his confirmation as a Supreme Court justice in 1916 [28] would be a far cry from the open tolerance he knew in the 1880s and 1890s. This freedom from stigmatization as a Jew allowed Brandeis to develop without a real need to prove himself as something other than what he was, and to live without the defensive sensitivities that he might be treading upon in places where he was unwelcome because of his race. Of all the prominent Jews of the early twentieth century, none had so little identification with Jewish life as he did, nor did any have so wide a network of Gentile friends and colleagues.

This lack of anti-Semitism can be traced at least in part to the old analogy of the Jews and the Puritans, each a "chosen people," one the inhabitors of the original Zion, the other the founders of a "Zion in the Wilderness." Hebrew had long been a staple in the Harvard College curriculum, and from 1630 on many Bay State residents had prided themselves on their learning in Hebraic studies. Jews had been in large measure exempt from the nativist sentiments of the 1840s and 1850s in New England, and their "genius" had been defended in a number of scholarly and sympathetic histories.[29] Even Henry Adams, who later held near-hysterical racist views, in 1880 had drawn a flattering portrait of Jews in his novel *Democracy*.[30] Many New Englanders had been incensed by the Dreyfus case (which seems not to have affected Brandeis at all), and when resort hotels had instituted a policy of excluding Jews, William James, among others, had determined to "return the boycott." [31]

Part of this tolerance may have been due simply to the lack of a large-scale Jewish immigration to Boston. What little

there had been consisted mainly of German Jews who had
come before the Civil War, and who had assiduously worked at
assimilation. They had been fairly successful, and, indeed, had
provided a model to which proper Boston could point with
pride. They greatly admired Solomon Schindler, the rabbi at
the leading Reform temple, and the Brahmins had flocked to
hear his assimilationist sermons.[32] Not until 1895 was it necessary to organize the various Hebrew charities, when large numbers of the "new" immigration from eastern Europe settled in
the poorer parts of the city.

Even Brandeis's opponents did not identify him as a Jew
until after he had gained national prominence, but by then a
bad case of xenophobia heavily tinged with anti-Semitism had
afflicted the caste-conscious Brahmins. He had not changed,
but they had. Even after he joined the Zionist movement, he
continued to think in terms that at one time had been familiar
to his Boston peers: "Zionism is the Pilgrim inspiration and
impulse over again; the descendents of the Pilgrim Fathers
should not find it hard to understand and sympathize with
it." [33] These words, at one time understandable to the Boston
élite, were in 1915 strange to the ears of both Jewish ghetto-
dwellers and Brahmins.[34]

The influence of Boston remained with Louis Brandeis all
his life, and he was always a little hurt and puzzled at how the
Brahmins had turned on him. Irving Katz has suggested that
Brandeis represented "reform," while his bitter antagonist, Colonel Henry Lee Higginson, represented the Brahmin "tradition." According to Katz, Higginson thought Brandeis "lacked
proper 'character' which proper Bostonians had inherited from
their antecedents. All that people like Higginson represented
and held dear—respectability, free enterprise, truth, character
—was now in danger of subversion by the evil, scheming
Brandeis." [35] It was Brandeis, however, who really stood for
"tradition," the older vital tradition of the pre–Civil War élite,
a tradition that expected and supported reform. Higginson, despite his undeniable talents, symbolized the declining caste

which, in its weakness, defensively closed in around itself, and raised to fetishes the symbols of its original vigor.

Brandeis did, after all, display in ample quantity all of the character traits that Higginson demanded.[36] His "respectability" had been evident to all, even Higginson, until 1907, as evidenced by his profession, success, and membership in the right clubs. As for "free enterprise," no one was a more unrelenting champion of the system, but here again, Brandeis harked back to the older tradition of independent merchants and farmers. "Half a century ago," he wrote:

> nearly every American boy could look forward to becoming independent as a farmer or mechanic, in business or professional life; and nearly every American girl might expect to become the wife of such a man. To-day most American boys have reason to believe that throughout life they will work in some capacity as employees of others, either in private or public business; and a large percentage of women occupy like positions.[37]

The financiers of the great consolidations had choked off opportunity for the small entrepreneur, and therefore, as Brandeis believed, were undermining the free enterprise system.[38] He fought not against the system, but against those who unwittingly were killing it. Here Higginson, despite his occasional vagaries, stood for the new—the "reform," if you will—of finance capitalism, which had relegated the individual to a subservient position; Brandeis remained true to the old tradition of independence.

Despite Higginson's accusations to the contrary, Brandeis's truthfulness and integrity have never seriously been questioned.[39] Brandeis insisted on telling the harsh truth, and frequently his analysis of these facts went against prevailing public opinion. His charges against the life insurance companies, and especially against the New Haven management, brought into question the reassurances of fiscal stability which the State Street Brahmins constantly issued. Could there be any better example of fiscal rectitude than that during the New

Haven battle, he urged Harvard to rid itself of New Haven stock in its portfolio, not because it was unsound (which it was), but because its management had perpetrated unethical practices! [40] Indeed, as far as the New Haven matter went, charges of truthlessness might more easily be proven against Higginson than Brandeis.[41]

If this is so, why then was Brandeis so vilified by Boston's finest citizens? The seeming answer would be that they resented his standing so firmly for the proud New England traditions, values whose meanings the Brahmins in their decline had perverted. Brandeis fought all his life for those values—honesty, justice, freedom, civic responsibility, public virtue, and individual opportunity. Like William Ellery Channing and William Lloyd Garrison, Brandeis drew down on his head the resentment of those whom he sternly called back to duty as he saw it. Higginson and the others could not understand that even while criticizing the new social order, Brandeis never questioned the validity of the old moral values; his greatness lay in his ability to apply them to new conditions.

Chapter II

THE LAWYER AND THE LAW

"My, how I detest that man's ideas. But he is one of the greatest technical lawyers I have ever known." [1] This remark by Mr. Justice Sutherland, an extremely capable lawyer in his own right, summed up much of the frustration that many of Louis D. Brandeis's critics felt. How had one so capable, so successful in the law—the very citadel of conservatism *—come to hold such strange notions regarding the state, the legal profession, laissez-faire, and other pillars of the established order? This perplexity can be resolved if, in the context of late nineteenth-century economic, social, and legal developments, we see Brandeis attempting not only to come to grips with these trends, but also trying to apply older ethical precepts to new and radically different situations. Despite allegations to the contrary by friend and foe alike, Brandeis was, in the Burkean sense of the word, deeply conservative.

* "Conservatism" and "liberalism" are extremely difficult words for historians to use with precision. Not only have these catchwords meant different things in different times, but they also have emotional connotations. The "conservatism" of those with whom Brandeis frequently clashed was less a defense of the past than an effort to freeze the present; conditions had changed drastically in a short time, and they desired to hold change in place. Brandeis recognized that severe alterations had occurred, but he believed in an older, more humanistic tradition, and he sought to allow just enough further change to reestablish the supremacy of human rights over property rights.

The era in which Brandeis earned his reputation as one of the greatest and most successful of American lawyers witnessed a near-revolutionary change in the social and economic makeup of the country. The forces unleashed by the Civil War had burst into full bloom with the peace. Railroad mileage had shot up from 36,801 miles in 1866 to 193,346 miles in 1900, while the freight carried had doubled and then doubled again. The gross national product in these years had increased twelve-fold, aided by the seemingly overnight creation of new industries in steel, oil, and mineral production. Values of exports from American mills and factories had climbed from $434 million in 1866 to $1.5 billion in 1900, while imports had more than doubled. To staff the new factories, millions of immigrants, especially from southern and eastern Europe, had come to this country. The only weak spot in the economy seemed to be agriculture, where the price index had slipped by 50 percent; yet even there, the total value of farm machinery and implements had tripled.[2]

This transformation from a homogeneous society based on a relatively simple, rural, small-unit economy into one characterized by complexity, urbanism, and industrialism affected not only the practice of the law, but its outlook as well. Much of the work the lawyer was called upon to perform in 1900 had hardly existed prior to the Civil War. The growth of big business based on the corporate form had caused commercial law, formerly a minute part of the general practice, to mushroom to become the bulk of the lawyer's workload, consuming most of his time and providing the greater part of his income. Not only did attorneys have to master the intricacies of stock issues, consolidations, bankruptcies, receiverships, and the like, they also had to come to grips with a growing governmental involvement with business affairs. The passage of the various granger laws, the establishment of the Interstate Commerce Commission in 1887, and the enactment of the Sherman Antitrust Statute in 1890 introduced a new set of rules—most of them vague—into business affairs, and lawyers had to work with rulings and in conditions for which their previous training and experience had ill-prepared them.

The effects of these developments upon the legal profession as a whole manifested themselves in several ways which are central to our understanding of Brandeis's importance. First, there was the shift in the lawyer's role from adversary to counsel. Second, the growing specialization and commercialization of lawyers led to a new type of practice and new duties for the attorney. Finally, a majority of lawyers welcomed and sustained a conservatism at bench and bar which attempted to freeze the status quo and which evaded the moral dilemmas of industrial change.

Prior to the Civil War, the legal profession had reflected fairly accurately the social fabric of the times. Law offices had been small, staffed by an attorney and one or two clerks, or, in some cases, by two or three lawyers who, if not in actual partnership, at least had shared office space and books. The problems they had dealt with had been fairly simple and had concerned not so much conflicting interpretations of fact as questions of the law. In that era, as Willard Hurst has noted, "Men still saw their relationships largely on a one-to-one basis (buyer-seller, lender-borrower, grantor-grantee); they had little familiarity with multicornered dealings; they had little sense of individual helplessness in the face of great impersonal social currents; they felt little awareness that the public might have concern with matters wholly 'private' in origin." [3]

It had been less a question of ignoring facts than that facts had been simpler and more easily understandable. The economic and legal intricacies of the later nineteenth century were absent, and the intelligent layman had understood the "facts" with as much clarity as had the lawyer. Moreover, men had come to lawyers only when all other recourse had failed and they were ready to fight. The duty of the attorney, then, had been to play advocate for his client, to make the best legal presentation possible. Given these demands, the best lawyers had been the generalists; in fact, there had been few specialists of any kind. A lawyer who had hoped to earn his living in an expanding frontier society had to be competent in such fields as land and water law, as well as civil and criminal procedures.

By 1870 all of this had begun to change, because the society at large had become more complex and could no longer live with a simple law. The one-to-one relationships gave way to multifaceted operations, and simple business had been overwhelmed by large undertakings. Now it could be too expensive to go wrong, too costly to call the lawyer at the last moment, too wearing to fight a battle that would be taxing even if won. More and more lawyers found themselves called in to advise clients on future actions, on what to do to avoid going to court. "A lawyer's chief business," said Elihu Root, "is to keep his clients out of litigation." [4]

This shift from advocate to counsel and the adjustment to the new requirements were both hesitant and painful. It was one thing to enter a case with all the facts available, and then sort out those which would be most helpful to the client's case; it was something else to guess what future events would yield. New modes of business operation required the lawyer to pay close attention to economic trends and to evaluate developments in which he was not expert. The creation of trusts and estates and corporate organizations called for planning and analysis of a large number of variables, including questions of economics, sociology, psychology, and labor, as well as business. The lawyer of the future, Holmes predicted, would not be the lawbook scholar, but "the man of statistics and the master of economics." [5]

The old-style generalist could normally handle almost any type of case. The postwar era saw the emergence of the specialist, first in commercial law as a whole, and then in the various aspects of it. Soon men devoted their entire careers to trusts or estates or receiverships or stock issues. Since big business needed all of these skills, the result was the growth of large offices, staffed with any number of specialists and subordinates, all working on corporate problems. [6] Some of the larger industrial companies even established law departments of their own, for reasons of both economy and convenience.

This division of labor may have made for better legal advice on particular problems, but it had severe limitations. Very few lawyers could see beyond their little niche to advise on larger problems. The earlier generalists had been admired as men of affairs; the specialists were not expected to know anything outside their narrow enclaves. Businessmen might seek their skills for specific problems, but not necessarily their advice on questions of overall policy. Soon industrial leaders stopped asking "What should I do?" with all its moral implications and started demanding "Tell me the best way to do this!" Lawyers thus abdicated their responsibility as moral instructors and confined their activity to devising the best way for corporate clients to effect certain ends, some of them of questionable legality. "Instead of being advisers, lawyers were collaborators in their clients' short-sightedness," declared Felix Frankfurter. ". . . The lawyers did their clients' bidding instead of illuminating their minds to understand something about the forces with which they were dealing." [7] The independent practitioner gave way to what many reviled as a "hired hand" working in a "law factory." "The practice of law," charged one critic, "has become commercialized. It has been transformed from a profession to a business, and a hustling business at that." An article in a leading law journal declared that the lawyer's motives "are as sordid and his activities as mercenary as can be found in any other occupation." [8] Obviously, not all lawyers rejoiced at the new modes of practicing law.

The needs of the lawyer in his roles as counsel and specialist should have made him more aware of the social and economic problems of the country, more receptive to new ideas, but they did not. Instead, the lawyers' new interdependence with business made them nearly blind to all demands except those of the corporate world. By the 1890s, an increasingly reactionary bench and bar had moved to block popular forces from imposing legislative restrictions on business activity. A creed of laissez-faire and freedom of contract had been erected by a majority of the legal profession as a totem second only, perhaps, to the Constitution. Building upon the foundation of the Fourteenth Amendment, lawyers and judges elevated the vested rights of property to heights previously envisioned only in Tory dreams. William Ramsey proudly proclaimed the new dogma to his fellow attorneys: "The right to contract and to be contracted with . . . is sacred, and lies at the very foundation of the social state." [9]

Property rights had always been an important part of the American heritage, and from the earliest settlements there had been a latent conflict, occasionally boiling to the surface, between human rights and the emphasis on property. In the years before the Civil War, these two forces had ridden in compatible, if not always easy, harness. After all, property protection affected not only men of substance, while democratic ideals could be found in all strata of society. But, at least in lip service, the society had normally placed human values above materialism.

The era that opened with Appomattox saw an economic growth unparalleled in human history, but a growth whose benefits were unequally distributed. While "captains of industry" like Andrew Carnegie and John D. Rockefeller, or just plain thieves like Jim Fisk or Daniel Drew, raked in millions of dollars, farmers saw their markets restricted and urban laborers lived in horrid slums at bare subsistence levels. Before the forces of a humane democracy could rally, the spokesmen for property had established a supremacy whose chief tenets, simply stated, were: the inviolability of property; governmental noninterference with economic matters; implied or expressed limitations on the legislative powers regarding business; freedom of contract; and the duty of bar and bench to defend this creed.[10]

Thus, when various state legislatures attempted to restrain some of the new industrialism's labor abuses, a series of cases in state and Federal courts quickly put them in their place. As Sidney Fine notes,[11] these cases followed a fairly similar pattern. Citing Field or some other eminent jurist,[12] the courts would define liberty and property to include freedom of contract. Since labor was a form of property, any efforts to regulate labor violated either the freedom and due process guaranteed by the Fourteenth Amendment or the sanctity of contract protected by Article I, Section 10, of the Constitution; since the laws frequently applied to workers in a particular industry, or to employers of a certain type, the statute would be doubly damned as vicious class legislation.[13]

Similar efforts to ameliorate other problems of the new industrial age also ran afoul of the courts. Congressional policy against monopolies was practically emasculated, while an income tax similar to one in use during the Civil War was declared invalid,[14] to the unanticipated glee of conservatives. "American constitutionalism," writes Arnold Paul, "underwent a revolution in the 1890's, a conservative-oriented revolution which vastly expanded the scope of judicial supremacy, with important consequences for American economic and political history." [15]

This reaction by the courts to social welfare programs and labor legislation was not a case of unconscious, ignorant rejection, but a deliberate program to establish permanently the propertied bias. From bench, bar, and academy, the refrain was constant: the legal profession had a special duty to perform. Stephen J. Field assiduously worked to turn his dissent in the Munn case [16] into court-accepted doctrine.[17] On the one hundredth anniversary of the Supreme Court, he declared unequivocally that the main business of that tribunal was enforcement of the property rights in the Constitution.[18] Many lower courts enthusiastically followed Field's lead and erected their own barriers to reform legislation.[19] In Wisconsin, Judge James G. Jenkins went so far as to prohibit workers not only from striking, but even from quitting their jobs, since this would infringe upon the rights of their employers.[20]

This attitude was reinforced at meeting after meeting of state and local bar associations. William Guthrie warned his colleagues of the "despotism of the majority." "We lawyers," he intoned, "are delegated not merely to defend constitutional guaranties before the courts for individual clients, but to teach the people in season and out to value and respect individual liberty and the rights of property. . . . Today, more than ever, the bar is the great conservative force in American politics." [21] John F. Dillon lectured the New York State Bar Association on "Property—Its Rights and Duties in Our Legal and Social System," and inveighed against the viciousness of the income tax.[22] From the academies, eminent scholars contributed their voices. In the most influential legal text of the period, Thomas McIntyre Cooley buttressed the doctrine of implied limitations on state powers and reinforced the growing concern for property rights.[23]

Judicial conservatism erected a wall of precedents to block future legislative reforms and to protect laissez-faire. Thus, at the same time that lawyers were forced into a greater awareness of social and economic change, the law itself was being locked into a one-dimensional view of reality. These two trends, however, were not necessarily contradictory. In times of rapid change, men often look to bulwarks of the past to sustain them until calmer times. The conservative doctrine had always been there; indeed, Locke had frequently equated property rights with human rights. Conservatives could now justify business practices (and abuses) by appealing to the latent materialism that had always hovered just below the surface. Lawyers had to know certain facts, it is true, but they did not have to evaluate them from a moral stance. All they had to do was utilize the facts while creating a doctrine of laissez-faire to hide behind. This approach well suited the so-called corporation lawyers and those who labored in the law factories, who saw themselves not as lackeys or glorified clerks, but rather as protectors of the American way.

Thus by the 1890s a fairly clear, though certainly not monolithic, pattern had emerged in the legal profession. From being primarily an advocate, the lawyer had begun to act as a counsel to his clients, and this required that he have a large amount of data available to him. With growing economic and social complexity, the practice of law had become specialized, providing greater competence in particular fields, but at a loss of the overall view. With an emphasis on commercial work, lawyers had become allied with businessmen in defending the latter's practices and abuses. At the same time, bench and bar had erected a protective wall built upon the principles of laissez-faire, property rights, and limitations upon the legislative power; with each decision, a new conservative legal philosophy rationalizing these developments had been strengthened. It is in this context that we must examine Louis Brandeis and his career as a lawyer.

From his youth, Louis Brandeis had loved the law. Originally inspired by his uncle, Lewis Naphtali Dembitz, a practicing attorney as well as a brilliant legal scholar,[24] Brandeis never regretted his choice of vocation. From September 27, 1875, when he entered the Harvard Law School, until February 13, 1939, when he retired as an associate justice of the United States Supreme Court, he gloried in the challenge and opportunity of the law.

Brandeis entered Harvard Law during one of its most exciting phases, and his instant infatuation with it shone through clearly in his letters home. "You have undoubtedly heard," he wrote to his brother-in-law, "how well I am pleased with everything that pertains to the law." "Law seems so interesting to me in all its aspects," he told his sister, "it is difficult for me to understand that any of the initiated should not burn with enthusiasm." Difficulties with his eyes only made him "look forward to the time when I shall again be able to satisfy my desperate longing for more law." [25] His enjoyment of the law, as well as his native brilliance, enabled him to compile a near-perfect record in his studies.

After graduation and a year's practice in St. Louis, Brandeis was easily lured back to his beloved Boston by his classmate, Samuel D. Warren. To offset living expenses in their first year, Warren had proposed that they take over the editorship of a legal periodical. While Brandeis agreed with the reasoning, he made clear that his first desire was to practice law. The editorship, he explained, "should not monopolize our time and we should have sufficient time to devote to the law business to enable us to work up a practice. For, although I am very desirous of devoting some of my time to the literary part of the law, I wish to become known as a practising lawyer [as opposed to a legal scholar]." [26] Later success would not dampen this enthusiasm. Well after his prominence had been recognized by all, he would write to his brother Alfred about his impatience during a quiet spell: "I really long for the excitement of the contest—that is a good one covering days or weeks. There is a certain joy in the draining exhaustion and backache of a long trial, which shorter skirmishes cannot afford." [27] Certainly this type of ego was better suited for the center stage of combat than for the quiet alcoves of a law library.

Brandeis's success as a lawyer rested on several grounds. First, there was his sheer brilliance and enthusiasm for the law. His phenomenal memory enabled him to recall nearly all the pertinent facts of a case, which he could marshal with a moment's thought. His wide reading frequently made him more knowledgeable on a subject than so-called expert witnesses. Time and again he would confound his opposition by knowing more about their business than they did. His handling of oral arguments, from various reports, was among the best of his time. Clients flocked to his office because, among other things, he was the top legal technician in the country.[28]

Brandeis, however, was more than a mere technician. In a period of transition from advocate to counsel, he was not only the best of the former, but a model of what the latter should and could be. In his advice to his clients, Brandeis went out of his way to know as many facets as possible of an issue; he had to know as much about a problem as did his clients, and then a great deal more. After all, why should they come to him unless his knowledge and perspective were greater than their own? In order to do this, he early determined that knowledge of details was essential, combined with an understanding of how men lived and worked. "Know thoroughly each fact," he noted. "Don't believe client witnesses. Examine documents. Reason; use imagination. Know bookkeeping—the universal language of business; know persons. . . . Know not only specific cases, but whole subjects. Can't otherwise know the facts. Know not only those facts which bear on direct controversy, but know all the facts and law that surround." [29]

Knowledge of law and detail by themselves would be useless, however, unless the attorney also understood the nature of men and of their businesses. Brandeis expounded on this subject at length to William Dunbar in 1893, when the younger lawyer, later to be Brandeis's partner, did not seem to be achieving the success at the bar that his intelligence and ability warranted. What makes Brandeis's letter to Dunbar so interesting is that it summed up not only the ingredients which were necessary for the lawyer's success, but also the qualities which businessmen were then seeking:

> Cultivate the society of men—particularly men of affairs. This is essential to your professional success. Pursue that study as heretofore you have devoted yourself to books. Lose no opportunity of becoming acquainted with men, of learning to feel instinctively their inclinations, of familiarizing yourself with their personal and business habits. Use your ability in making opportunities to do this. . . .
>
> The knowledge of men, the ability to handle, to impress them is needed by you—not only in order that clients may appreciate your advice and that you may be able to apply the law to human affairs—but also that you may more accurately and surely determine what the rules of law are, that is, what the courts will adopt. You are prone in legal investigation to be controlled by logic and to underestimate the logic of facts. Knowledge of the decided cases and of the rules of logic cannot alone make a great lawyer. He must know, must feel "in his bones" the facts to which they apply—must know, too, that if they do not stand the test of such application the logical result will somehow or other be avoided. . . .
>
> The man who does not know intimately human affairs is apt to make of the law a bed of Procrustes. No hermit can be a great lawyer, least of all a commercial lawyer. When from a knowledge of law, you pass to its application the need of a full knowledge of men and of their affairs becomes even more apparent. The duty of the lawyer today is not that of a solver of legal conundrums; he is indeed a counsellor at law. . . . Your duty is as much to know the facts as law—to apply from your own store of human experience the defects in the clients' statements and to probe the correctness of those statements in the light of your knowledge. . . .
>
> But perhaps most important of all is the impressing of clients and satisfying them. Your law may be perfect, your ability to apply it great and yet you cannot be a successful advisor unless your advice is followed; it will not be followed unless you can satisfy your clients, unless you impress them with your superior knowledge and that you cannot do unless you know their affairs better than they because you see them from a fullness of knowledge. . . .[30]

Still another element of Brandeis's success was his organizing ability. No man could be both generalist and specialist amid the growing complexities of an industrialized society, not even Brandeis with his wide-ranging knowledge and familiarity with practical affairs. So he built a large firm, staffed by men learned in the law and in facts, and supported by a capable clerical staff; and while he never approved of narrowness, he did encourage specialization. He served as a catalyst to pull his subordinates into a working organism. As Edward McClennan noted, it was really the firm, rather than any of the partners, which practices law. Again to Dunbar, Brandeis explained the necessity of a large firm:

> *First:* The organization of large offices is becoming more and more a business—and hence also a professional necessity. If properly planned and administered, it must result in the greatest efficiency to clients and the greatest success to the individual members both pecuniarily and in reputation.
>
> *Second:* In such an organization the place of each man must be found—not prescribed. The advantage of the larger field is that every man has the opportunity of trying himself at everything or anything—and by a natural law comes to do those things that on the whole he does most effectively.
>
> *Third:* As to that class of things which the individual makes his own, he must become in the office in time the principal—for those dealing with the office learn that he is considered the authority there on those things. . . . In other words a reputation in the practical world to which the practice of the law belongs is determined by a large number of qualities and in a proper organization they have even better scope for effectiveness today than in individuals standing alone.
>
> *Fourth:* Besides the things to which the individual becomes the principal there must be always much as to which he is the associate, the Junior or Senior of the others in the organization and every man must stand ready to give every other man full aid. . . . That such organizations are the most effective means of doing the law work of this country—so far as clients are concerned—is proven by the success of the great New York firms. . . .[31]

Here, perhaps, is the one place where Brandeis felt that bigness might be a virtue, although his own personality and priorities kept his firm, at least while he headed it, from becoming a law "factory."

By any number of standards, Brandeis enjoyed great success at the bar. His large practice, the number of important clients who sought his advice, and his standing among his colleagues proved this. In terms of monetary achievement, he ranked among the top six moneymakers at the Boston bar, and in the top group in the country as well. In 1890, at the age of thirty-four, he earned more than $50,000 a year, while 75 percent of the lawyers in the country made less than $5,000 annually. In 1912, when he was already devoting much of his time to public work, he received over $105,000 from his law practice. By frugal living and conservative investment, at a time when there was no income tax, he accumulated his first million by 1907; he accumulated another million before he went on the Court, and died leaving an estate of more than $3,000,000.[32]

Many other lawyers shared some, or perhaps even all of these traits in greater or lesser degree. What made Brandeis different from other successful lawyers of his day is that he not only mastered the changes that were occurring in the legal profession, he saw beyond them to the problems of the greater society; few other lawyers looked past their little professional niches. These differences, centering about his belief that the law and life could not be artificially separated, are what made Brandeis a great lawyer. In an age of specialization, he refused to be trapped by narrowness. Moreover, he felt obligated not only to be counsel to his clients, but to serve the public as well, and in serving it, educated it by illuminating all that he touched.

The growing wall between law and social progress aroused opposition within the profession on the part of other attorneys besides Brandeis. In the 1890s, as Arnold Paul notes, the "legal progressives," although a minority, commanded some respect and could occasionally influence moderate conservatives.[33] Although the progressive–conservative alignment within the profession shifted constantly as a result of various strains and stresses, at no time did Brandeis stand alone in opposing the artificial climate of conservative decisions and statutes made without concern for the hard facts of economic and social developments.

Oliver Wendell Holmes, Jr., had attacked the conservatives in 1880 in his Lowell Lectures on the common law. In the past, he declared, "the felt necessities of the time, prevalent moral and political theories, [and] intuitions of public policy" affected the growth of the law more than the so-called legal logic upon which the reactionaries relied to block social reforms.[34] Appointed to the high court in 1902, Holmes continued to lend prestige and inspiration to other progressives through his powerful dissents.[35] Allan Brown in 1892 had accused the Supreme Court of thwarting the people and had endorsed popular election of judges to "keep them in touch with the people," and the same year Conrad Reno had castigated the courts for following outmoded concepts irrelevant to the times.[36] Although Brandeis could not secure an invitation to present a paper to the American Bar Association on the responsibilities of lawyers to the public, his two most important speeches concerning the legal profession were published in prestigious journals.[37]

In these speeches, Brandeis spelled out his belief that the law had not kept pace with the times, and he raked the conservatives for their blindness. "Political as well as economic and social sciences," he declared,

> noted these revolutionary changes. But legal science—the unwritten or judge-made laws as distinguished from legislation—was largely deaf and blind to them. Courts continued to ignore newly arisen social needs. They applied complacently eighteenth-century conceptions of the liberty of the individual and of the sacredness of private property. Early nineteenth-century scientific half-truths like "The survival of the fittest," which, translated into practice, meant "The devil take the hindmost," were erected by judicial sanction into a moral law. Where statutes giving expression to the new social spirit were clearly constitutional, judges, imbued with the spirit of individualism, often construed them away. Where any doubts as to the constitutionality of such statutes could find lodgment, courts all too frequently declared the acts void.... The law has everywhere a tendency to lag behind the facts of life.[38]

Was it any wonder, he asked, that there had been so much resentment and dissatisfaction with the law and with the courts,
when legal institutions "had not kept pace with the rapid development of our political, economic, and social ideals." [39] He
quoted approvingly Lowell's words:

> New times demand new issues and new men,
>   The world advances, and in time outgrows the laws
> That our fathers' time were best;
>   And, doubtless, after us some purer scheme
> Will be shaped out by wiser men than we—
>   Made wiser by the steady growth of truth.[40]

When Brandeis suggested that legal justice could no
longer be equated with social justice, he may have considered
that the great cultural lag in the common law had called equity
jurisdiction into being. Legal progressives maintained that the
real vitality of the law lay in its approximation of the needs of
the people; the law must serve as a repository of the rules and
maxims by which people live. While the law always lagged
somewhat during periods of change, new needs, as Lowell
wrote, had eventually called new laws into being, laws reflecting not a cold science, but Holmes's "felt necessities." The new
laws reflected accommodations already made by the people. In
the late nineteenth century, the lag was more pronounced than
usual, and when the people (acting through their legislatures)
attempted to close this gap, they found their way blocked by a
wall of court decisions.

While there had been activist courts before (notably during the tenures of John Marshall and Roger Taney), there had
also been a strong tradition that the legislative branch, since it
most directly represented the people, should not be overruled
except for a clear violation of some Constitutional proscription.
Now using the tools of the sanctity of contract clause and the
Fourteenth Amendment, the courts were blocking substantive
reforms, interposing their will over that of the legislatures, and
thus creating a judge-made law.

Brandeis frequently quoted the old maxim that "out of
the facts grows the law," and he insisted that only when the

courts obeyed this rule could they hope to achieve freedom from popular dissatisfaction. A good example, he declared, had been the Illinois courts in the two Ritchie cases.[41] In the first Ritchie case, "the court, reasoning from abstract conception, held a limitation of working hours to be arbitrary and unreasonable; while in the second Ritchie case, reasoning from life, it held the limitation of hours not to be arbitrary and unreasonable. In other words, in the second Ritchie case it took notice of those facts of general knowledge embraced in the world's experience with unrestricted working hours, which the court in the earlier case had ignored." [42]

Throughout his career, Brandeis preached this doctrine. In 1891, in one of his first public causes (arguing for a more realistic liquor law), he had lectured the Massachusetts legislature that "No law can be effective which does not take into consideration the conditions of the community for which it is designed." [43] To a Congressional committee two decades later he repeated the message. "In all our legislation," he argued, "we have got to base what we do on facts and not on theories." [44] On the bench, he would never lose sight of the old common law maxim. "The logic of words," he would warn his brethren, "should yield to the logic of realities." [45] As Paul Freund has written, Brandeis "developed his larger conception from immersion in the facts of specific cases, in the best tradition of the common law. That tradition is not unlike the methods of scientific discovery, which abstracts general truths through reflection on a mass of scientific phenomena." [46]

To breach this chasm in his own life between life and the law, Brandeis refused to limit his interests. At a time when many of his colleagues locked themselves into a specialty, he practiced the whole field of law. "From the outset," wrote his partner, "the practice which came to him was a general one, unusually diversified. It did not fall into a single class. It broadened rather than narrowed with the lapse of time. He acted for manufacturers, for merchants, for investors, for brokers, for associations of these different ones, for labor unions, for the injured, for the successful, for the unsuccessful, and for benevolent institutions. There was no field not included unless it be in the defense of prosecution for alleged criminals, the department of patents, and admiralty. Even in these unaccustomed fields he worked occasionally." [47] He would not fall victim to "the cost of vast areas of ignorance and [the] grave danger of resultant distortion of judgment" which he warned specialization would bring.[48] Perhaps one reason he turned to public causes is that they gave him the opportunity to enjoy his individualism as well as to operate in a broad framework.

Brandeis's role as counsel rather than advocate overarched limited areas. What made him so effective was his ability to see all the sides of an issue, and then advise his clients on the best overall approach to head off possible trouble. Interestingly enough, this objective attitude was one of the chief charges against him in 1916, when his opponents claimed that he had failed to be enough of an advocate; his judicial attitude as counsel, they maintained, disqualified him for the role of an associate justice of the Supreme Court.[49]

His work as counsel took a variety of forms. At first, he advised primarily his private clients, many of whom ranked among the leading businessmen of New England. He would listen to their troubles, digest as much data as possible, and then try to get them to understand the problem from an overall viewpoint rather than from their own parochial stance. The best-known example, of course, occurred when William H. McElwain, head of a large shoe manufacturing company, called on Brandeis to secure his help in some labor problems. McElwain wanted his employees to accept a wage cut; times were bad, he insisted, and his workers had previously been paid a very high rate. By steady questioning, however, Brandeis soon discovered that nearly every worker, through no fault of his own, suffered long layoffs during slack periods. The high wages for working days, combined with the layoffs, yielded a miserable annual wage. To overcome this, Brandeis suggested that McElwain reorganize and rationalize his business by securing his orders well in advance of delivery. He could then run his factory on a regular basis, spacing orders to fill in heretofore slack times. McElwain accepted the advice, to the benefit of his employees as well as his stockholders.[50] Another time, a successful businessman suddenly decided that he wanted to go into the ministry and sought Brandeis's advice; the lawyer's suggestion was that the work of God might better be done by an experienced merchant running his shop on a humanitarian basis than by a novice cleric. The man was convinced.[51]

This desire to see all the sides of a problem, to be counsel to the situation rather than just to the client, and to be independent, eventually led Brandeis into his public career as people's attorney. He agreed to represent a liquor lobby only after he had secured their consent to let him tackle the larger problem of liquor control. When a client, the Wisconsin Central, had to be reorganized, he personally assumed responsibility in order to secure a fair representation of all parties. In perhaps the best-known case, E. A. Filene brought Brandeis into the 1910 garment workers' strike to try to arrange a solution. The lawyer had the trust and respect of both employers and employees, and the solution he eventually proposed, the preferential shop, seemed eminently fair to everyone. In various rate cases, the Interstate Commerce Commissioners called on him to advise them of the overall implications, while other lawyers fought to present only their clients' cases.

Few lawyers at that time engaged in any sort of public service work. When successful attorneys did take time out for "good works," they usually devoted their efforts to professionally acceptable labors involving technical reform of the law, through the Commissions on Uniform State Laws and, later, the American Law Institute.[52] The idea of serving the public directly, however, had entered into very few minds. When the city of Philadelphia fought a corrupt gas company, it could not even hire a local attorney to handle the case and had to go to New York to secure legal representation.[53] Brandeis was the most conspicuous of a small handful of lawyers doing *pro bono publico* work.

He himself noted this lack of public service, and several times called it to the attention of his colleagues. "Instead of holding a position of independence, between the wealthy and the people," he asserted, "able lawyers have, to a large extent, allowed themselves to become adjuncts of great corporations and have neglected their obligation to use their powers for the protection of the people. We hear much of the 'corporation lawyer' and far too little of the 'people's lawyer.' The great opportunity of the American Bar is and will be to stand again as it did in the past, ready to protect also the interests of the people." [54] He especially took to task those who pursued practices for the protection of business that they would have condemned had they viewed the problems strictly as citizens. The lawyer would have to maintain his integrity if he hoped to recapture the respect of the people.

Brandeis drew a clear distinction between work for a private client and counsel in a public cause. While his legal fees were appropriately commensurate with the quality of his work for his clients, he soon determined not to accept payment for public work. When Edward A. Filene tried to get a bill from him for service during a traction fight, Brandeis put him off continuously. Finally, in exasperation, Filene bearded him in his office. He later wrote that Brandeis "told me he never made a charge for public service of this kind; that it was his duty as it was mine to help protect the public rights; and when I remonstrated, saying that he and his family were dependent upon his income, he told me that he had resolved early in life to give at least one hour a day to public service, and later on he hoped to give fully half his time." [55] During the controversy over consolidation of the Boston gas companies, the Commonwealth hired Charles Palen Hall as special counsel, although Brandeis dominated the hearings and negotiations. Hall recognized this and wanted to divide the $2,000 fee with Brandeis. The People's Attorney stoutly refused, although, he added to Hall, "if it will relieve your mind I shall not object if a small part of it goes to the Public Franchise League. But that is the utmost limit to which you can change my assent." [56]

His "exquisite moral susceptibility" [57] would not allow him to stop there. He recognized that as he gave less time to his firm's work and more to public service, his firm's income would suffer as a result. Although none of his partners ever even suggested it, Brandeis insisted upon paying the firm of Brandeis, Dunbar & Nutter for the privilege of using his time for public service. "I do not think," he explained, "that my partners and others interested in the profits of the firm ought to be affected by my own feeling in this matter [the New Haven merger], and I therefore wish to substitute myself as the client of the firm in this matter so far as charges for my own services are concerned." [58]

This unusual practice aroused a great deal of comment, and time and again reporters asked Brandeis why he did it, why work for the public at all, instead of making donations to worthy causes. His answer on one occasion is worth quoting in full, since it gives us a rare glimpse not only at the lawyer doing *pro bono publico* work but also of the man. "Some men buy diamonds and rare works of art," he began; "others delight in automobiles and yachts. My luxury is to invest my surplus effort, beyond that required for the proper support of my family, to the pleasure of taking up a problem and solving, or helping to solve, it for the people without receiving any compensation. Your yachtsman or automobilist would lose much of his enjoyment if he were obliged to do for pay what he is doing for the love of the thing itself. So I should lose much of my satisfaction if I were paid in connection with public services of this kind. I have only one life, and it is short enough. Why waste it on things I don't want most? I don't want money or property most. I want to be free." [59] For Brandeis, "the great happiness in life [was] not to donate but to serve." [60]

This answer gives us a glimpse into the nature of a man who would forsake a lucrative private practice for the public arena of the "people's attorney." Brandeis was preeminently a twentieth-century man in many ways: as a technician, he was attracted by the intricacies of solving complicated problems; in a complex society, he esteemed the role of playing honest broker to all sides and parties to an issue; his faith that a critical examination of empirical evidence could lead to social progress was shared by many progressive reformers; his desire to rationalize business and to utilize corporate power for public good marked many "corporate liberals." Yet underneath the twentieth-century man was the eighteenth-century individualist: a

Puritan who believed in the therapeutic value of work for its own sake; the individualist who would not be submerged in a mass society; the generalist who preferred the overview to specialization (even while rationalizing specialization in his own law firm); the citizen insisting that service to the public was part of every man's obligations. It is this conflict in Brandeis's psychological makeup that provided the impetus for his turning to reform, and it also is the clue to his success. He adopted modern techniques and imbued them with an old-fashioned ethos. Just as his economics reflected his morality, so did his law; in both he sought to be free.

Before Brandeis would take on a case, public or private, he had to be sure of the moral soundness of his position, a characteristic that set him apart from other lawyers. The adversary system of justice assumed, and still does, that any case coming to court must have some legal backing, and therefore some right, on both sides. The purpose of lawyers was to present their client's case and persuade either judge or jury that their client had a better, or more just, argument than their opponents. The defects of this system showed up plainly as more and more lawyers moved from the role of adversary to that of counsel; it played down the weighing beforehand of the relative merits of both sides, and it allowed lawyers who were mere technicians to evade moral problems by the assumption that some right existed on any side.

Brandeis both in his public and his private work would act only when he believed in the legitimacy of his clients' cases. When men came to him who were clearly in the wrong, he would tell them so, and try to get them to see that their best interests in the long run would be to do the right thing. When one of his clients went bankrupt, Brandeis agreed to assist the family only after they had pledged that they wanted the fairest settlement possible for their creditors.[61] Even the normal practices of the bar were not sacred when he believed them wrong, and as a young attorney he had angered many of his colleagues by attacking a cost-reimbursement feature of one case.[62] As David Levy points out, Brandeis by his example asked lawyers to start making moral judgments and to stop turning their backs on complex situations. In a 1907 address, he declared: "What the lawyer needs to redeem himself is not more ability or physical courage but the moral courage in the face of financial loss and personal ill-will to stand for right and justice." [63]

Finally, Brandeis emphasized the role of the lawyer and of the law as an educational instrument. Before the lawyer could instruct the courts and the public, however, he would have to learn a great deal himself. The distorting effects of intense specialization, he predicted, could be corrected "by broad education—by study undertaken preparatory to practice—and continued by lawyer and judge throughout life." [64] The lawyer could serve as the conduit through which life and the law would be kept in contact, and Brandeis constantly emphasized the need for "fitting the lawyer and the judge to perform adequately the function of harmonizing law with life." [65]

The job of so educating lawyers fell primarily on the law schools, and here perhaps Brandeis relied overmuch on his own rewarding experience at Harvard.[66] He had been fortunate to have studied there during the ferment of Langdell's reform; there he learned not only the principles of the common law, but he also saw the weaknesses as well as the strengths of the case method. From 1886 on, he had been active in various affairs of the School, had taught a course there, and had urged upon Dean Langdell and President Eliot the necessity for courses more closely related to everyday affairs.[67] In 1912, he listed as a prime factor in improving the legal profession a better education for lawyers. "This involves," he wrote, "the socialization of legal education, and that in turn requires that lawyers should not merely learn rules of law, but their purposes and effect when applied to the affairs of man." [68] The lawyer who did not study sociology and economics, he warned, "is very apt to become a public enemy." [69] Brandeis himself, as one adversary noted, was one of the few lawyers of his time who understood finance as well as law.[70]

But the lawyer had to recognize that even beyond his own education, his responsibility lay in educating the public and the courts to social realities. As early as 1900, Brandeis had urged lawyers to voluntarily assist state legislators in reviewing proposed laws, in order that legal principles and social needs be in harmony.[71] Quoting Matthew Arnold's statement that "lack of recent information is responsible for more mistakes of judgment than erroneous reasoning," he declared that the lawyer's special duty was to provide that information. "A judge rarely performs his function adequately," he noted, "unless the case before him is adequately presented." [72] Instead of lecturing on the sanctity of the contract, Brandeis pleaded with his colleagues to teach the courts and the public the facts of life in an industrialized America.

It is in this context that we must view Brandeis's strategy in the case of *Muller v. Oregon*.[73] For decades, reformers, lawyers, and scholars have lauded Brandeis's "radical" brief, with its two pages of legal citations and over one hundred pages of labor statistics.[74] I would suggest, however, that the real brilliance of the Brandeis brief lay in its attempt to harmonize the law with the need for social progress. The great strength of the law is its proximity and relevance to life, and in *Muller* Brandeis prodded the law into the first step on the road back to that relevance.

Brandeis had been approached by his sister-in-law, Josephine Goldmark, and by Florence Kelley, on behalf of the Consumers League, to defend an Oregon law establishing a ten-hour workday for women.[75] He agreed to do so on two conditions: first, that he officially represent the State of Oregon in court and not just serve as *amicus curiae* for the League; and second, that the League provide him with a massive amount of data on the effects of long working hours on women. He had spotted a loophole when the Supreme Court had invalidated a similar New York statute in 1905.[76] In that case, the Court, while striking down a ten-hour day for bakers, had allowed that the police power of a state could be invoked if legitimately warranted. Other lawyers had failed to see that the Lochner decision did not have to be overturned; one had to establish a legitimacy by proving a factual connection between the law and the conditions of life which had invoked it, and not through legal syllogisms.

In many ways, *Muller* was a crucial point in Brandeis's life. On the one hand, he was now attacking the highest bastion of legal conservatism; if he lost there, the law would be even more separated from life than it had been, and the old guard even more firmly in control. On the other hand, all that Brandeis had stood for in his own career was also at stake, and if he lost, the development of a legal philosophy in which lawyers committed themselves to protecting the general, rather than the corporate, welfare would be retarded. And, needless to say, his own reputation was involved. On *Muller,* as on few other cases of this era, a great decision hung in the balance. Not only the fate of the Oregon statute, but the development of the legal profession and the path of the law would also be affected.

The ten-hour law struck at a vital tenet of the conservative creed, the so-called liberty of contract. If a person wanted to work 12 or 14 or even 18 hours a day, and could find someone willing to hire him, then both parties were "free" to contract such an arrangement. While this reasoning may have been valid in earlier, simpler times, the Industrial Revolution had undermined one of the premises on which it rested—the supposed equality of both contracting parties. A village blacksmith and his hired hand might have stood roughly as equals, but certainly no parity existed between the United States Steel Corporation and an unskilled laborer, a "fact" that the law had failed to notice. The Oregon statute declared, in effect, that if all parties to a contract were not equal, then the state under its police power could limit the right to contract in order to protect its citizens.

This the conservative lawyers could not concede. Joseph H. Choate, a pillar of the New York bar, declared that he could not understand why a big strong husky laundrywoman should not work more than ten hours a day if she so wanted.[77] He and others feared that if this restriction on the "liberty to contract" were allowed to stand, other restrictions—on hours for men, working conditions, and even wage minimums—would soon be enacted. The laissez-faire philosophy demanded that no matter how unequal the game, no interference by the

state could be allowed. Equality before the law was thus carried
to its logical, yet patently unfair, extreme.

In the *Muller* case, Brandeis brought together several of
the themes that had concerned him—and other legal progressives—into a unified whole, and the case illustrated the main
tenets of his legal philosophy. He did more than argue the
case as advocate for Oregon; he tried to get all sides to understand why the state had passed the law, and why it was a necessary statute. He advised the Court, and in doing so, lectured
the learned justices on matters of which they knew little, yet
which were essential to their understanding of the case. Long
before *Muller*, Brandeis had written, "A judge is presumed to
know the elements of law, but there is no presumption that he
knows the facts." [78] After *Muller*, lawyers could never again
evade the responsibility of instructing and advising the courts
about the relevant facts. As Felix Frankfurter later noted, after
this case such a task became a prime responsibility of counsel.[79]

All sides of the case also involved the opposition, and
Brandeis hoped that they too would listen to what he had to
say. He did not care for governmental intervention any more
than they did and feared overmuch regulation as harmful to a
free society. But he knew that the greater the opposition to
minimal social progress, the greater would be the popular demand for more extreme measures. As counsel, he was advising
those who would freeze the status quo that it was an impossible
task and recommending that they learn to live with what had
to be. The need was real and would be met, eventually, by the
law; it would be better if men of good will cooperated in ame-
liorating the inequities of industrial transition.

No mere technician could have written the brief that
Brandeis did. Granted it took a dedicated researcher to dig up
that material, but the thousands of shards of evidence that Miss
Goldmark had frantically gathered were transformed into a
whole, a logical and consistent statement of man's accumulated
wisdom on the subject of long working hours for women. He
then had to educate lawyers, not in legal syllogisms, but in a

simple fact: women were different from men.[80] Here the educator took over, to instruct one and all on what the law should be, and more importantly, why it should be that way.

The triumph of *Muller* is that the Court began to recognize what Brandeis had always preached: that the life of the law lay not in dusty precedents or in syllogistic reasoning; that the society would not be saved by trying to freeze one moment in its history; but that law and social needs had to go together. It would be another thirty years before the full triumph implicit in the *Muller* case would be secured, and there would be many setbacks on the way.[81] But after 1908, the law began to accommodate itself to the needs of social change, rather than serve as a barrier to progress.

Chapter III

THE ECONOMIST
AS MORALIST

D espite the fact that problems of industrialization lay at the core of the progressive ferment in Brandeis's time, few of the reformers really developed well-thought-out programs to tackle the economic questions that confronted them. A significant exception was Brandeis, who, despite a lack of formal training in economics, articulated a philosophy concerned with the major issues of his time. In speeches, articles, letters, and testimony before various Congressional committees, he explored the relationships that linked giant private economic powers, state and Federal governments, and the public welfare. Brandeis relied upon what he conceived of as the basic American principles of an open competitive society, in which private interests yielded to the public good. The key to understanding his economic program, however, is the recognition that economics, like the law, must be governed by immutable moral rules.

Before the latter part of the nineteenth century, Americans for the most part had not paid much attention to—or been bothered by—economics. Although issues of economic importance had arisen, such as the tariff, land policy, public works, and railroad expansion, these items had been as much political as economic, and their resolution had usually accommodated political interests, interests which fortunately had co-incided with the economic needs of the nation. Indeed, eco-nomics and politics had always been thought about together, and men like John Adams, Alexander Hamilton, Thomas Jef-ferson, and Albert Gallatin had never tried to theorize strictly about economics. They had seen, long before Marx, how closely the country's political framework related to its economic base.

What little theorizing had occurred reflected that of the classical European school, which emphasized laissez-faire, free competition, and the absence of monopolistic enterprises. Al-though the English common law had originally curtailed mo-nopolies primarily for the protection of merchants, eighteenth-century theorists had opposed them in order to protect the consumer. "The price of monopoly," Adam Smith had declared unequivocally, "is upon every occasion the highest which can be got. . . . The price of free competition, on the contrary, is the lowest which can be taken." [1] In addition to competition, the classical economists had also posited the self-regulating na-ture of a free economy. According to Jean Baptiste Say's "Law of Markets," the act of producing goods generated the necessary purchasing power to buy them; as long as the purchasing power was used, the value of production always stayed in equi-librium with buying power, precluding serious depressions or inflations. A third assumption of these writers had been open access to and egress from the market. High demand would in-duce new producers to open business. Eventually their produc-tion would cause prices to find a natural level, as well as to sate the demand. If price was above equilibrium, demand would be greater than supply; if below equilibrium, then the least effi-cient manufacturers would close down until equilibrium would be restored.

Americans, however, had added a moral ingredient to this classical mix. The free market also provided a testing ground for the strength of a man's character and ability. The Protes-tant Ethic combined with a rawboned frontier spirit to pro-duce a curious amalgam of free competition, moral striving, and the pitting of man against nature. Out of this came the belief that all men deserved an equal opportunity to make the most of their abilities. Those who succeeded commanded respect and admiration, while those who failed were ignored; and any restrictions on this opportunity—either to curb the strong or to help the weak—were condemned as immoral. Moreover, the open-ended nature of America's society and economy allowed such free access, and provided examples of such rapid progress, that success soon became an ingrained part of the formula. It became an article of faith that any man with a little capital could open a business and prosper, and that even men without money could make good. A young man who had hired out for wages yesterday, went the saying, works for himself today, and tomorrow will hire others to work for him. While we cannot know how often fact bore out faith, there is little doubt that the faith was common at the time.

In the decades following the Civil War, the American economy underwent drastic changes. By the end of the nineteenth century, free lands had for the most part disappeared. A flood of immigrants had alleviated the chronic labor shortage, and more and more men now worked for other people with little hope of ever owning their own businesses. As the manufacturing processes became more complex, access of new producers grew restricted; it now frequently took large amounts of capital to establish new plants. The most ominous trend, however, lay in the consolidation of small units into large enterprises with monopolistic or near-monopolistic control over their particular markets.

Between 1898 and the end of 1901, 2,274 firms disappeared as a result of mergers, and merger capitalization totaled $5,409,000,000.[2] In the steel industry, the various mergers dominated their fields: American Tin Plate held 75 percent of the country's capacity in that product; American Steel and Wire, 80 percent; National Tube, 85 percent; and American Bridge, 50 percent. All of these firms, plus several more, joined together in 1901 into the United States Steel Corporation. Capitalized at well over one billion dollars, U.S. Steel brought under one control 213 different manufacturing plants and transportation companies, 41 mines, 1,000 miles of private railroad, 112 ore vessels, 78 blast furnaces, as well as the world's

greatest coke, coal, and ore holdings. It controlled 43.2 percent
of the nation's pig iron capacity, and 60 percent of basic and
finished steel production.[3] Under the domination of a John D.
Rockefeller, the Standard Oil conglomeration demonstrated
how easily a monopoly could drive small, independent operators out of business.[4]

Suddenly the gap between belief and practice widened.
Perfect competition had been the basis of academic theory;
men now debated how the new industrial economy affected the
traditional beliefs in free markets and equal opportunity. By
the turn of the century, the pros and cons of an economy dominated by large industrial units exercising great power formed
the central problem of popular American economic thought.

Building upon the classical base of laissez-faire, with a
small admixture of conservative Darwinism, the defenders of
big business and monopoly maintained that giant corporations
had resulted from "natural causes," and that to interfere with
their operations would not only hinder progress, but would adversely undermine the strength of the American economy. S. C.
T. Dodd, one of Standard Oil's lawyers, praised the technical
superiority of consolidated operations, and described them as
the catalytic agents of change in "the march of civilization." [5]
As to firms elbowed aside on this "march," the apologists of
bigness dismissed them as weaklings, and their demise as a necessary price to be paid for progress. In John D. Rockefeller's fa-
mous analogy, they were the weak shoots which had to be
pruned to allow the full blooming of the American Beauty
Rose.

The moral strain of this chorus appeared constantly in the
emphasis laid on the strength of character of the so-called captains of industry. Time and again, Rockefeller, Andrew Carnegie, E. H. Harriman, and James J. Hill were epitomized as the
models of self-made men, who had built their empires upon
skill and good character, men whom every schoolboy should
emulate.[6] The darker side of their success—the shady dealings,
the squalid slums spawned by factories, the cruel working
conditions—frightened many people, but, as John Garraty
notes, this only increased the veneration and public obeisance

to the older virtues, the "continuing veneration of individualism, self-reliance, and *laissez-faire* economics." [7]

Certainly the belief in laissez-faire constituted an essential
component of the pro-business argument. While accepting subsidiary help in the form of road-building, protective tariffs, and
land grants for railroads, the business community almost unani-
mously agreed that governmental restraint would constitute interference in the natural laws of economics and would
inevitably produce disaster.[8] The very thought of the government protecting the public from supposed hardships inflicted
by the giant combines aroused the hackles of industrial leaders.
People learn and profit from hardship, declared Henry O. Have-
meyer, president of the American Sugar Refining Corporation. "Let the buyer beware; that covers the whole business.
You cannot wet nurse people from the time they are born
until the time they die. They have got to wade in and get
stuck, and that is the way men are educated and cultivated." [9]

Business apologists diverged to some extent over the merits of competition. Many economists and business spokesmen
still believed in unfettered competition as a principle of economic law, one which would equalize production and distribution. According to classical doctrine, competition would keep
prices at their natural, lowest level, thus benefiting the consumer while assuring a fair, but not unjust, price for the producer. Moreover, competition was the medium through which
character was tested. As late as 1916, after the government had
already taken a few halting steps to limit the power of big business and to regulate competition, a leading financial journal attacked the idea of helping small business at all and accused the
Federal Trade Commission of coddling "the slow, instead of
bidding him raise his head and use his own powers." The glory
of competitive success would be spoiled if the government tried
to preserve the incompetent.[10]

But while bold and speculative entrepreneurs like Andrew
Carnegie might welcome the hazards of free competition, new
leaders of giant corporations shifted their emphasis from competition to cooperation for the sake of market stability. The
mad scramble for markets in the 1880s and 1890s had con-

vinced many businessmen that irrational competition was, in the end, extremely damaging. Under the leadership of men like George W. Perkins of the House of Morgan, Elbert H. Gary of U.S. Steel, Cyrus H. McCormick of International Harvester, as well as John D. Rockefeller, Jr., a new system of business thought developed which Arthur Jerome Eddy, its chief theoretician, called "The New Competition." [11]

Ideally, the "New Competition" would provide industry with market stability, so that long-term prices would not fluctuate greatly. In times of prosperity, the price level would rise only moderately, while in slack periods it would not drop very much at all. In place of cutting prices and other "unethical" practices, businessmen would emphasize quality and service to their customers, while cooperating with other members of the industry in sharing information and in self-regulation. A stable market, price maintenance, and improved service would benefit both producer and consumer, while theoretically harming no one. In many ways, the "New Competition" faced up to the fact that in basic manufacturing industries, plant costs were too great for easy access of newcomers and investment too large to allow frequent business closures. It also recognized that in a complex industrial society, consumer, producer, and laborer were too interdependent even to contemplate erratic fluctuations in the market.

While business apologists developed their arguments, opposition to big business also grew. Long before the antimonopoly emotion crested in Woodrow Wilson's 1912 campaign, serious observers had begun questioning whether the supposed benefits of the new industrialism outweighed the increasingly obvious disadvantages. Although surfacing periodically in various political campaigns and magazine articles, the antimonopoly sentiment had failed to develop into a cohesive movement or to find an articulate leader prior to 1900. Increasingly, however, a large number of thoughtful men came to view big business as inimical to a democratic society. They objected in particular to oppressive business practices, the unduly concentrated wealth and power of the new industrial giants, and governmental practices which favored the giants.[12]

This protest took a variety of forms, ranging from proposals for limited and specific reforms to utopian visions of a reconstituted society. Henry George, for one, enjoyed a long vogue with his doctrine of a single tax, which would recover to the state all unearned and unjustified increments on land, and scores of Single-Tax Leagues spread across the country.[13] Frank Parsons, reflecting Owenite antecedents, devised a philosophy of "mutualism" as a basis for a cooperative society based on brotherly love, in which production would be controlled by worker cooperatives and the government run by social engineers.[14] Various politicians espoused schemes to limit the size of companies or to place special taxes on big business. A growing concern with conservation of natural resources added another dimension to the antimonopoly movement, since the big corporations and railroads were frequently the greatest despoilers of the environment. Many conservationists believed and preached that the common heritage had fallen under the control of vested interests to the detriment of the general welfare.[15]

The anxieties aroused by the growth of large and powerful corporations forced a reexamination of hitherto accepted economic beliefs and led many businessmen as well as their critics to at least a partial rejection of laissez-faire. But if many people were willing to admit some form of governmental intervention in the economy, there was still a great debate over what form that intervention should take. At one extreme, men argued that the government ought to run all business; at the other stood the diehards who opposed each and every contact between business and government. The continuum between the extremes included a number of combinations of private initiative with federal regulation. Few of the proposals were as well developed, however, as the plan to use the powers of the federal government to reestablish and then regulate competition, and the chief advocate of this philosophy was Louis Brandeis.

The milieu of reform, discussed in the first chapter, had one glaring weakness, and that was its failure to keep abreast of changing economic values. Up to 1880, an undergraduate at

Harvard College could not take a course dealing with the impact of the Industrial Revolution. He might compete in an essay contest on the "Metayer System of Farming," but no one seemed interested in teaching the effects of the factory system upon people. What little political economy existed echoed the orthodox dogma of the classical school, which viewed the factory as an unmixed blessing and assumed that laissez-faire was the Eleventh Commandment. According to Francis Amasa Walker, later the president of the Massachusetts Institute of Technology, laissez-faire during these years "was not made the test of economic orthodoxy, merely; it was used to decide whether a man was an economist at all." [16]

Although Massachusetts led the nation in the adoption of factory codes and other laws designed to protect the working people, the good people of the Commonwealth seemed unwilling fully to come to grips with the basic social problems, fully to examine the relationships between the factories and slums and diseases. They could console themselves with the laws that reformers had pushed through, and with stories of how well the Lawrence family treated the girls working in its mills. The bankers of State Street, busy consolidating their fortunes or financing new enterprises, did not worry about the elimination of small companies by the new giants. Small firms, after all, did not issue stocks and bonds.

Brandeis was never economically ignorant. Economic matters were discussed within the family, and he had the example of his father, a successful grain and produce merchant. Adolph Brandeis was able to dissolve his business at the first signs of the Panic of 1873 and take his family on a three-year trip to Europe. This foresight and thrift impressed young Louis enormously. He never personally felt the harsher side of economic life; while others had gone bankrupt, his father had gone on a grand tour. Although his family could not pay his way through Harvard Law, his brother did have enough to lend him to give him a start; he earned the rest through tutoring. When he graduated, he had not only paid all of his expenses and repaid the loan to Alfred, but also had accumulated over $1,200 in savings.

Brandeis never really questioned the basic rightness of the American system of free enterprise; that it had its defects he was prepared to admit, and he did a great deal to formulate proposals on how these should be corrected. His own success, however, imbued him with a sense of the great opportunities awaiting the hard worker; if the demands were great, so proportionately were the rewards. He differed with many of his fellow reformers in Boston when he insisted that risk capital deserved greater returns than capital invested in safe measures, although he condemned outright speculation. Despite his advocacy of such measures as savings bank insurance and wage and hours regulation, Brandeis cannot be said to have greatly concerned himself with the weak. Those who competed had to bear the losses as well as enjoy the victories; he would back measures which prevented the strong from taking advantage of the weak, but not those which tried to give a leg up to those on the bottom. The competition of life, of the economy, with both the harshness and the rewards, was always acceptable to him; life itself should not be easy, but a challenge.

Brandeis inherited from his father a belief in putting all of one's eggs in one basket, and then, as Andrew Carnegie once said, watching that basket very closely. He explained his beliefs in moneymaking and investment to his brother, at a time when both were quite prosperous:

Father also talked to me about your stock purchases. I dare say those you have made are all right, but I feel very sure that unser eins [people like us] ought not to buy and sell stocks. We don't know much about the business, and beware people who think they do. Prices of stocks are made. They don't grow; and their fluctuations are not due to natural causes. Altogether, I don't think John Taussig [Alfred's brother-in-law] knows any more about them than most other bankers who are outsiders. And even the Insiders could not be relied upon for advice.

My idea is that your situation is about like mine, namely, to treat investments as a necessary Evil, indulging in the operation as rarely as possible. Buy only the thing you consider very good, and stick to it unless you have cause to doubt the wisdom of your purchase.

And when you buy, buy the thing which you think is
safe, and will give you a fair return; but don't try to make
your money out of investments. Make it out of your business.[17]

Brandeis never trusted the stock market and made nearly all of
his investments in safe railroad or municipal bonds. The few
times that he bought stock were usually connected with his law
practice; he had to own a few shares to attend stockholders'
meetings or to sit on a board of directors. The idea of making
money for its own sake, especially through a system that
smacked of gambling, repelled him; the only value of money
lay in that it gave him the freedom to do the things he wanted
to do. "I believe in investing money where it will be so safe,"
he said, "that I will not have to take time off thinking about
it." [18]

The inequities of stock manipulation never ceased to
anger him, and he constantly inveighed against the notion that
people could get something for nothing. "Arithmetic," he declared, "is the first of sciences and the mother of safety." [19]
Eventually, therefore, all attempts to violate basic rules would
end in disaster, and he wondered why people would not recognize this. In part, he suggested, investors had been deluded by
get-rich-quick schemes. "Large dividends," he explained to a
Senate investigating committee, "are the bribes which the managers tender the small investor for the power conferred to use
other people's money." To wage war against the corrupt and
powerful bankers was only part of the problem; unlike most reformers, Brandeis stood willing to lay a large part of the blame
for manipulation on the small purchasers, the ones who frequently screamed loudest when expected profits failed to ma-
terialize. "To my mind," he went on:

> there is no such thing as an innocent purchaser of stocks. It is
> entirely contrary, not only to our laws but to what ought to be
> our whole attitude toward investments, that the person who
> has a chance of profit by going into an enterprise, or the
> chance of getting a larger return than he could get on a per-
> fectly safe mortgage or bond—that he should have the chance
> of gain without any responsibility. The idea of such persons

being innocent in the sense of not letting them take the consequences of their acts is, to my mind, highly immoral and is
bound to work out, if pursued, in very evil results to the community. When a person buys stock in any of those organizations of doubtful validity and of doubtful practices, he is not
innocent; he is guilty constructively by law and should be
deemed so by the community and held up to a responsibility;
precisely to the same responsibility that the English owners of
Irish estates have been held up, although it was their bailiffs
who were guilty of nearly every oppression that attended to
the absentee landlordism of Ireland.[20]

Brandeis's attacks on the money manipulators, best seen
in *Other People's Money, and How the Bankers Use It*,[21] constituted but one phase of his critique of American enterprise.
While others either embraced the new economy, or rose in fear
against it, he was one of the few who attempted to understand
and explain what he objected to, and to propose a solution.
One of the elements of his greatness is that he never attacked
an evil just to destroy it, but always sought to put a better alternative in its place.

Brandeis's central thesis claimed that political freedom depended upon individual financial independence, and that industrial giantism—the curse of bigness—threatened that freedom. To defend this argument, Brandeis did much more than
marshal a large array of statistics to prove that big business
dominated the nation's economy; he returned to older ideals of
freedom to substantiate his claim that bigness in a democracy
contradicted the very tenets of a free society.

Brandeis started with the assumption that the best possible
socioeconomic framework for a democratic society was one
based on a small-unit economy, that is, one in which the bulk
of productive and distributive work was done through small
agencies—independent farmers, merchants, manufacturers, and
so on. The division of wealth, labor, and responsibility among as
many people as possible assured to each not only a voice, but
also a stake, in the growth and stability of the society. Brandeis
greatly admired Jefferson, and like him, drew a portrait of a
nation of independent yeomen, shopkeepers, and artisans. He

yearned, naïvely perhaps, for a return of the day when "nearly every American boy could look forward to becoming independent as a farmer or mechanic," [22] not out of nostalgia, but out of a belief that opportunity of this sort was essential to free and democratic processes.

Time and again he emphasized that individual opportunity was an essential of political freedom. "You cannot have true American citizenship, you cannot preserve political liberty, you cannot secure American standards of living," he informed the Senate, "unless some degree of industrial liberty accompanies it." [23] The social costs of the displacement of small businesses by huge corporations, by absentee ownership, and by banker control worried him much more than the new economic order. The domination of large and uncontrolled trusts presented a grave danger to democracy.[24] If people no longer felt they controlled their own economic destiny even in part, then the traditional basis of the political structure would be threatened. Employees could be coerced, especially if they worked for gigantic companies, and if more and more people became employees, with no hope of independence, then the possibility of business control over the political processes grew great indeed. "There cannot be liberty without financial independence," he argued, "and the greatest danger to the people of the United States today is in becoming, as they are gradually more and more, a class of employees." [25]

The argument that the growth of large corporations represented a fundamental and irrevocable law of economic development did not impress him, nor did he accept the monopolists' claims that the industrial giants operated more economically than did small companies, and could thus provide all Americans with a higher standard of living. This "offer" missed the entire point of what America meant. "It is absolutely essential," he agreed, "in order that men develop that they be properly fed and properly housed, and that they have proper opportunities of education and recreation." A free nation demanded no less. But, he went on, "we may have all these things and have a nation of slaves." [26] The issue involved priorities of values: Did we, as a nation, want to have material comfort or freedom?

Industrial giantism undermined democracy not only from the threat of corporate influence, but also from the counterforces it generated. "The talk of the agitator alone does not advance socialism a step," he warned, "but the formation of great trusts . . . with the attendant rapacity or the dishonesty of their potent managers and their frequent corruption of councils and legislatures is hastening us almost irresistibly into socialistic measures. The great captains of industry and finance, who profess the greatest horror of the extension of governmental functions, are the chief makers of socialism." [27] He frequently tried to impress upon the businessmen with whom he came into contact that the preservation of free enterprise rested not on ruthlessly crushing those who opposed them, but by recognizing their legitimate grievances, and then cutting the ground out from under them by correcting these ills voluntarily. Brandeis wanted the government to do as little as possible here; voluntary associations, with legislative sanctions, worked best, and his chief exhibit was the savings banks selling industrial insurance. Those who urged the government to right all wrongs, he believed, were as dangerous as those who opposed any governmental action at all. To strike that balance required individual businessmen to operate their companies honestly, economically, and properly, a feat he considered the trusts incapable of performing.

Brandeis recognized that merely pointing out the political dangers of big businesses would be insufficient to halt their growth or to arouse the public consciousness against them. So he set out to demonstrate that the technical arguments in support of bigness were unsound. Competition among relatively small units, he maintained, constituted the most efficient means of producing and distributing the nation's goods. That there might be some waste in this type of economy he did not deny; but again he raised the question of values. Which type of waste, and what consequences, did the country desire least? "The only argument that has been seriously advanced in favor of private monopoly is that competition involves waste, while monopoly prevents waste and leads to efficiency," he wrote. "The argument is essentially unsound. The wastes of competition are negligible. The economies of monopoly are superficial and delusive. The efficiency of monopoly is at best temporary. Undoubtedly competition involves waste. What human activity does not? The wastes of democracy are among the greatest obvious wastes, but we have compensations in democracy which far outweigh that waste and make it more efficient than absolutism. So it is with competition." [28]

The reason behind Brandeis's charge of inefficiency in big operations rested on his belief that the ability and judgment of the person in charge constituted the single most important element of business success. As firms grew too large, they became unmanageable, because one person could no longer direct them well. Delegation of authority and responsibility in companies like U.S. Steel struck him as exceedingly poor business procedure. Obviously, Brandeis did not insist that all businesses be one-man operations; he recognized that some people did certain jobs very well, that others could supervise well, and that individual talents differed. His own law firm was organized on these principles. But once a company grew so big that the man in charge operated three or four removes from production, then that man really did not know what was happening. "Man's work often outruns the capacity of the individual man," [29] he wrote, and his faith in democracy began and ended with his faith in individual man.

Because he clothed his attack on industrial giantism in the language of scientific management, it should not be thought that he opposed bigness only on grounds of efficiency. His main complaint was essentially moral—that big business posed a threat to humane and democratic values—but he adopted the monopolists' own criteria as the chief spearhead of his own attack. Bigness, in any form, struck him as morally reprehensible.

Later on, during the New Deal, the growth of the federal bureaucracy upset him deeply, and for similar reasons. In a conversation with Alfred Lief, Brandeis explained that smallness and decentralization should extend to all aspects of American life and government. "The United States is too big to be a force for good," he declared. "Whatever we do is bound to be harmful. We have bitten off more than we can chew. Good can come from small countries. The United States should go back to the federation idea, letting each state evolve a policy and develop itself. There are enough good men in Alabama, for example, to make Alabama a good state. But the tendency is to put responsibility upon the federal Government. Each country should try—each community should try—to become a microcosm. That is how the people will develop. I am dead against the American idea of concentrating and specializing in one area. Communities growing wheat should also have mills." [30] This fascination with the possibilities of a small country led him to defend ardently the choice of Palestine as a home for the Jews. Palestine was the right size for great things to happen there.[31]

Thus the "curse of bigness" was not limited just to economic enterprises, but to undertakings of all sorts, public and private. Big government could be as bad as big business, because both violated the same rules of equality. In limited units, men could function and be on top of their jobs, and the public would be well served; in big units, men could not control their organizations and everyone would suffer. Moreover, big government created just as much a social threat as did monopoly. "We risk our whole system," Brandeis declared, "by creating a power which we cannot control." [32] That power, obviously, could be of any sort, economic or political, and a danger no matter who wielded it.

To correct these ills, Brandeis proposed restricting the growth of big business and cultivating more enlightened relationships among employers, employees, and the community. He believed that the growth of big business had resulted from unrestrained, cutthroat competition, in which the strongest— although not necessarily the most moral—had survived. (He did not, however, recognize or understand mergers that were technical in origin.) Restraints upon unethical business practices had to be instituted, he felt, to ensure fair competition between firms.[33] If a company failed as a result of the poor quality

of its product or improper management, then the economy and
the community gained; if businesses were forced out by illicit
means, then the community suffered.

Following his belief that bigness was inefficient, Brandeis
proposed that a natural limit existed on the size of companies,
and that businesses should not exceed that limit. "There is in
every line of business a unit of greatest efficiency," he wrote.
"The unit of greatest efficiency is reached when the disadvantages of size counterbalance the advantages. The unit of greatest efficiency is exceeded when the disadvantages of size outweigh the advantages." [34] The limitations of man to manage
properly more than a finite amount of work accounted for this
natural limit, for to Brandeis the success of any undertaking
depended upon the abilities of the directors. As long as they restricted themselves to what they could handle well, they would
prosper; beyond that, they had either to fail or to compensate
by adopting illicit methods of competition.

Brandeis's faith in the efficiency of small units led him to
become an ardent advocate of scientific management. In part,
he supported this movement to eliminate waste; his puritan
conscience abhorred waste. More importantly, he hoped that
scientific management would prove the greater efficiency of
small firms over large ones and would establish the point of
maximum economy. He had recognized that the limit on size
—if it existed—would vary from industry to industry, from
firm to firm, and even from time to time. He had been unable
to be more precise, and expected that some day a scientific
means would be devised to locate these elusive boundaries. But
he never despaired that a limit did, in fact, exist, and that to
exceed it invited disastrous social consequences. Years after he
went on the Court, he still hoped that such measures could be
devised. He urged Harold Laski to "spread further the truth
that progress must proceed from the aggregate of the perfor-
mances of individual men—and that each is a wee thing, despite the aids and habiliments with which science, invention,
and organization have surrounded him." The cult of efficiency
must secure "the wisdom and ingenuity to adjust our institu-

tions to the wee size of man and thus render possible his growth and development." [35]

Scientific management, in its broader implications, would also contribute to easing tensions among workers, employers, and the community, since it would increase productivity, and then assure a fair distribution of that increase. Brandeis considered it of vital concern that the worker and the community benefit from new production methods and other inventions of social and economic usefulness. While the entrepreneur undoubtedly should be compensated—and compensated fairly—for his risks, his innovation, and his capital, a fair and even generous return was all he should get. If profit reached exorbitant levels, that meant the workers were underpaid for their contributions, and the public was paying too much for the goods or services it had purchased. But in none of this did Brandeis suggest any fundamental changes in either the economic system or the power relationships.

Brandeis strove for a partnership among employer, employees, and the community. "A manufacturer stands today in a relation to employees," he had written in 1895, "not of master but of associate." [36] In his mediation in the New York garment strike and in setting up worker participation plans for several of his clients, he had tried to teach both employers and employees that theirs should not be an adversary relationship, but one of cooperation. If the company did not make money, jobs would be lost; if the owner did not treat his workers fairly or pay them well, then productivity, service, and profits would decline. He constantly urged his clients to inaugurate profit-sharing plans, since if a workman felt—even in the slightest way—that he owned a portion of the business, he would work that much harder.

Similarly, the community at large had a vital stake in the manner in which businesses, especially public service corporations, operated. The general well-being of the community depended upon business prosperity, but again, a *fair* prosperity. Large dividends on watered stock robbed the public of its wealth; a too stringent control on profits undermined the economy. The community had rights which had to be protected. When the Boston Elevated sought a long-term franchise lease at what Brandeis considered unfair rates, he opposed the plan, and lectured the legislature: "We are here to see that control rests with the community, that the Elevated Railway Company or any company that serves us . . . is the servant and not the master of the public." [37]

Brandeis, along with so many other progressives, did not fear capitalism and wanted as few regulations as possible governing the economy.[38] He parted company with many of his colleagues in the Public Franchise League in the fight over the consolidation of the Boston Gas Company. Where they saw the issue strictly in terms of limiting the capitalization in order to secure low rates, he viewed the matter as one of fairness to all parties concerned. Eventually, he put across the idea of a sliding scale, whereby the company could raise its dividend only if it simultaneously reduced its rates to the public. He reasoned correctly that the consumers would not object to the company making more money if, at the same time, service improved and rates declined. Within two years after passage of the bill, gas rates in Boston had been reduced 20 percent, while stock dividends rose from 7 to 9 percent. The agreement, Brandeis explained, "creates in effect a partnership between the community and the public service corporation," one that "may well be the beginning of an entirely new movement in America toward presenting an alternative to either municipal ownership or the strict corporate ownership." [39]

The essential element in Brandeis's approach to economic problems was his belief that new economic developments had to be at all times reconciled with the traditional values of a democratic society. An advocate of efficiency, he never confused his priorities; if competition and democracy were more "wasteful" than monopoly and absolutism, they still provided other benefits too important to lose. If big business adversely affected social ideals, then the economy should somehow be modified to alleviate the problem. The public welfare had to take precedence above all other considerations; freedom was too precious a commodity to lose.

Yet, unlike some of the antitrust advocates, he also kept a sense of perspective and understood that if too strong an industrial-financial coalition could threaten democracy, too weak a business structure could also pose a danger. He considered a free enterprise system part and parcel of the democratic society, and although industrial problems had to be solved, the basic structure seemed good. He had as little use for those who would be unjust to business as he had for the Wall Street operators manipulating other people's money. "Capital must be protected," he said, "in order to protect the community." [40]

Today, more than a half-century after the progressive crusade against the trusts, the rhetoric of economic criticism has changed greatly. While we still cling to the tradition of equal market access for individual operators and still trumpet the openness of free enterprise, the main issues confronting us are how a triad of gigantic powers—big business, big labor unions, and big government—can properly manipulate the economy so as to eliminate, or at least cushion, the vicissitudes of a free market. Although we still react with indignation at collusive efforts to grab a market, antitrust suits to break up big consolidations are almost a thing of the past. While we pay homage to the successful businessman, the way the capitalistic system provides or fails to provide a moral proving ground concerns us very little. The economic domination of *Fortune's* top five hundred supercorporations is less important than the performance of those firms. While politicians continue to investigate monopolistic practices, their emphasis is on correcting abuses rather than eliminating monopolies. The federal government in recent years has blessed many mergers in the name of greater service and efficiency. Even Ralph Nader, who is the nearest thing we have to a "People's Attorney," wants more control over the conduct of big buiness rather than its elimination. Occasional well-publicized antitrust suits are aimed at collusive disregard of public welfare rather than at the extent of market control. For all practical purposes, the antitrust crusade is dead, and bigness is rarely referred to as a "curse."

The growth of big business is now regarded by many historians and economists not as a deliberate design of economic imperialists, but as a necessary adjunct of the growing complexity and urbanization of American life. Small units operate at the peak of their efficiency when they provide or distribute goods in a relatively simple and uncluttered setting. A picturesque rural village may be the best locale for a smithy, a butcher, or a shoemaker; the market he serves is limited and the bulk of the goods and materials he needs are close at hand. But, as Alfred Chandler has shown, the growth of big cities made this type of small-unit enterprise obsolete and impractical. A butcher who slaughters his own meat has to have access to cattle on the hoof; even with refrigerated apparatus, he can provide meat for a limited population for only a short period of time. Considerations of health and traffic just do not allow herds of animals to be driven through city streets two or three times a week to slaughterhouses in every neighborhood. As a result, large-scale meatpacking firms located outside the cities, with retail outlets serving different neighborhoods. The development of refrigerated railroad cars allowed these companies to locate closer to the cattle ranges and extend their retailing operations over a national scale. The growth of giant enterprises like Armour or General Mills resulted from the market needs of an urbanizing society and not from design; to undo such growth would require the deurbanizing of the nation.[41]

Another consideration in the growth of big business is the demand, as apart from the nature, of the market; in a number of market situations, concentration may be the natural working of the market and not a subvention of it.[42] Technological change can overnight destroy a competitive market, even if the rival firms can quickly duplicate or adopt the innovations. Moreover, as products become more complex, ease of entry by new competitors becomes more difficult. It is one thing to open a small grocery or shoe store with a minimal amount of cash; it is something else to start a new steel mill or automobile factory. According to John Galbraith, new markets are really open only at the very beginning, when products are new and venture capital available to all; within a short period of time, the market will be dominated by the best, and access cut off from all other would-be entrants.[43]

Interestingly enough, the largest companies—those which Brandeis supposed suffered most from the inefficiency of bigness—have actually proven themselves to be the most innovative and in many cases the most efficient.[44] Part of the problem of Brandeis's argument concerning the ability of large companies to perform well stemmed from his moral belief in the superiority of the individual. Despite his advocacy of scientific management, he never allowed himself to believe that new administrative structures might perform best in large settings, or that they would develop a life and efficiency of their own, the "waste" involved having a socially redeeming value.

Much of the difficulty lay in the inability of anyone, including Brandeis, to devise an accurate measure of the limits of greatest efficiency. Despite his declaration that such a limit existed and that the country knew enough about industry to determine what that limit should be, no one could establish with certainty at what point a company reached its greatest effective size. Economists, in positing a principle of diminishing returns, once declared that optimal production size was reached when marginal cost equaled marginal revenue—that is, when the cost of producing one more unit equaled the return on that unit, then maximum profit had been reached. Producing beyond this point found the marginal cost greater than marginal revenue, and thus unprofitable to the company. On this basis, Brandeis's statements should have found an easy manner of implementation.

Economists, however, developed more sophisticated theories as the economy grew increasingly complex. The marginal cost/marginal revenue analysis is accurate for simple industries and still holds valid for most service industries. But the real markets in which giant corporations operate do not lend themselves so easily to a one-dimensional chart. Real markets are not diagrams, but a convoluted interacting of a large number of variables. If, in a certain market, one factor is doubled, then the profit may decrease; if three factors are doubled, the margin of profit may jump fourfold. In such cases (which are the norm and not the exception), an increasing return to scale favors bigness rather than moderation in size. As a rough rule of thumb, the greater the capitalization required, the larger the optimal size of a company, both geographically and financially.

Brandeis also wrote at a time when innovation did not play the major role in industry that it does today. One of his clients like Robert H. Ingersoll could produce basically the same watch, year in and year out. His profits were clear, and he did not have to maintain a research staff. Operating in this market, as a matter of fact, he had no margin for research at all. Every company kept its price as close to a competitive level as possible, and to build in a research cost would have pushed the price out of line competitively. Moreover, in simple products, innovation can be quickly copied, which means the inventor can enjoy a competitive advantage only for a brief period. Again, the more competitive and "pure" a market is, the less motivation or reward for innovation.

The result has been that nearly all major inventions and product innovations in the last fifty years have come not from small, competitive firms, but from the industrial giants. How many companies could afford to spend $27,000,000 over a thirteen-year period developing a single product, as DuPont did with nylon, before producing a single bolt of the miracle fiber? Research and development is a costly time-consuming process which can only be indulged in by big companies that operate in a market not beset by the fluctuations of competition, or at least the type of competition held dear by so many of the progressives. To put it bluntly, the more restricted a market, the greater the opportunity for innovation. "There can be little doubt," states Galbraith, "that oligopoly, both in theory and in fact, is strongly oriented toward change. There can be no serious doubt at all that the setting for innovation, which is so favorable in this market structure, disappears almost entirely as one approaches the competition of the competitive model." [45]

The reason for such an emphasis is that, contrary to earlier predictions, the elimination of "pure" competition has not resulted in the elimination of competition at all, but merely shifted it around into new modes. Several critics have suggested that part of the progressive problem is that they could not differentiate between the preservation of competition as a principle and the preservation of competitors.[46] As big business grew and markets became oligopolistic, competition in many cases actually increased. The emphasis shifted away from price competition to better service and product differentiation. The results have been administered prices by so-called price leaders, which allow all companies to operate at a safe profit margin and still have sufficient money left for research, development, and other functions.[47]

Brandeis would probably have answered that these and other criticisms of his economic philosophy were irrelevant. To him, the economic system might be the base of the social and political structure, but it had to remain subservient to the accepted political ideals. Once the society allowed the economy to take on a life and justification of its own, to achieve an importance in its own right, to determine political and social policies, then trouble loomed ahead. To a moralist, nonmoral considerations are secondary; to Brandeis, the economic and technical arguments for bigness were insignificant compared to (as he saw it) the democratic need for smallness.

As an economist, Brandeis thus spoke primarily as a moralist. Once we understand this we can see that the "curse of bigness" did not refer only to the size of big businesses; he worried about the effects that large-scale undertakings would have upon the individual. Did we as a nation want to have our business controlled by a few men? Did we want our children to grow up with no prospects save that of working for an impersonal monolith? Did we want the economic power of big business to undermine our political institutions? Or did we wish to try, for at least a little while longer, to preserve the type of society we had known before, a society where the scale of accomplishments remained geared to human rather than corporate needs?

It would be unfair to view Brandeis as a narrow-sighted defender of an anachronistic philosophy who refused to come to grips with the imperatives of a new era. As many people have noted, few of the progressives ever attempted to deal with the problems of a new industrialized society in as rigorous and systematic a way as he did. The difference is that the rest felt they had to accept the new industrialism and then accommodate their beliefs to its demands; Brandeis, almost alone, argued that industry must obey the requirements of a democratic society. He measured industrial needs against his view of human freedom, and found it lacking. What he wanted other Americans to do was to stop and to think about the costs of industrialization in terms of individual opportunity and political change, and to determine how much of this price they would willingly pay.

We have obviously not attempted to impose upon American industry the stringent controls and limits that Brandeis would have wanted; even in war time we have never really curbed business interests. It may have been too late to do so by 1912, and we will never know if regulated competition would have worked or not; certainly the pale echoes of it found in state and Federal regulatory agencies provide no fair indication. Only this remains certain: In a nation dedicated to the value of the individual, any form of corporate dominance—be it industrial, governmental, or union—poses a threat to a free society.

Chapter IV

WILSON, BRANDEIS, AND
THE TRUST ISSUE, 1912-1914

"**B**ecause Brandeis understood the problem thoroughly, because he was ready with a definite plan for the bridling of monopoly, he became the chief architect of the New Freedom." So writes Arthur Link, who credits Louis Brandeis with almost singlehandedly persuading the President to adopt an antitrust program that ran counter to Wilson's original thoughts.[1] Historians have long acknowledged Brandeis as a key, although discreet, figure in the Wilson Administration; the foes and many friends of the New Freedom considered him the *éminence grise* behind the presidential chair, and Wilson himself publicly acknowledged that he often turned to Brandeis for advice.[2] Yet for all the currency of the belief in Brandeis's influence, there has been little effort to explore or understand their ralationship, to see how Brandeis served as the "chief architect" of the New Freedom. The key can perhaps be found in the exchange of ideas over the major issue of the Progressive Era— the trusts. To understand the appeal of the Brandeisian approach, it is necessary to examine briefly the development of Wilson's economic thought.

Wilson, after a steady rise through the academic ranks, had burst upon the national scene as a reforming president of Princeton. In 1910, thanks to the efforts of Colonel George Harvey and New Jersey boss James Smith, Wilson had captured the Democratic nomination for governor. The conservative rulers of the Democracy believed they had named a man safe on economic dogma, but midway through the gubernatorial campaign they discovered they had caught a Tatar. Wilson, stoking the newly glowing embers of an old political ambition, realized that if he were to win he would have to become progressive.

By this point Wilson had moved away from an earlier economic conservatism to a questioning of the American system as it then stood. Wilson—the student, the professor, the college president—had for the most part believed that progress meant rightness: what survived was good. As a youth he had read E. L. Godkin's *The Nation*, Burke, Cobden, and Bright, and in so doing imbibed the purest of orthodox economic theory. In his economics courses at Princeton, Wilson had absorbed the doctrines of laissez-faire and governmental noninvolvement, as well as the importance of morality in business, doctrines most congenial to the young Calvinist. In his graduate years at Johns Hopkins, Wilson veered away from a strict Manchesterianism toward a more historically inductive view of economics. In the 1890s, according to William Diamond, Wilson began to speak and write in economic language which sanctioned some government action in the interest of society.[3] Yet as late as 1908, Wilson condemned any sort of government regulation as socialistic in principle, and sure to be followed by government ownership. As for the trusts, during this early period he praised them for "adding so enormously to the economy and efficiency of the nation's productive work" and blasted the Populist attack on them as socialistic. In a "Credo" written in 1907, he described trusts as the "most convenient and efficient instrumentalities of modern business," the vast bulk of whose transactions were legitimate.[4]

But around 1907 a new strain began to emerge, a strain based upon Wilson's stern Protestantism. As Richard Hofstadter perceptively pointed out, Wilson represented, above all, a middle class which viewed the economic system, not just as a means of production and distribution, but also as a moral system to reward certain desirable traits. Success in business rewarded energy, efficiency, morality, frugality, perseverance, and ambition; competition was the means by which one exercised and tested these traits. As more and more of American business became organized, less and less room remained for the individual to compete. Wilson spoke for a middle class being squeezed out by big business; he spoke, essentially, for the young men "on the make" with no room to rise.[5]

By the time he ran for governor in 1910, Wilson had accepted many of the basic premises regarding monopoly that were then being expounded by the muckrakers. But what could be done about trusts? Big business was here to stay, and with big business came many evils. Perhaps evil could be combated by moral force, by dragging corporate evil into the spotlight of public opinion. In one interview, he suggested that much of the furor over business could be eliminated if corporate meetings were open and subject to public scrutiny; executives would not do wrong if their sins were open for all to see. He would play on this theme time and again, emphasizing the individual's obligation to control his actions in the light of an absolute standard of morality. Wilson's secular concept of sin was selfishness and his speeches often referred to the dichotomy between action and morality. In dealing with monopoly, Wilson tended to attack individuals as the cause, rather than economic conditions. When he finally won the Democratic nomination, he had no other solution to offer regarding the problem of trusts than to establish a rule of justice while enforcing the Sherman Act's criminal provisions.[6]

Despite this vagueness in Wilson's thinking, Brandeis recognized that they both sought essentially the same things: a society free from the domination of either big government or large private businesses, with a competitive, small-unit economy offering opportunity to those who had the skill and the courage to venture forth. Politically, Brandeis originally supported the presidential aspirations of his good friend, Senator Robert M. LaFollette of Wisconsin, with whom he had worked on antitrust legislation. After LaFollette's collapse from nervous exhaustion in early 1912, Brandeis began to look more closely at the New Jersey governor. By the time Wilson won the nomination, Brandeis had decided to support him, and he wrote to LaFollette: "It seems to me those Progressives who do not consider themselves bound by party affiliations ought to give Wilson thorough support, not only to insure his election, but to give him all the aid and comfort which he will need to maintain the Progressive Position which he has assumed and to carry out the Progressive policies." [7] A few days later he came out publicly for Wilson, to the regret of several of his friends who had hoped he would support Theodore Roosevelt. But, as he confided to Norman Hapgood, the new party was primarily a Roosevelt group, and only afterward a Progressive party.[8] Soon after came an invitation to Sea Girt, Wilson's summer home.

Brandeis had written to Wilson on August 1, congratulating him on his proposal for tariff reduction. Wilson seized the opportunity to confer with the People's Attorney, and sent word through Charles R. Crane that he wished to meet Brandeis. An appointment was arranged, and on August 28 the two men ate lunch and disscussed the issues of the 1912 campaign for over three hours. When they emerged from the meeting, reporters crowded around, wanting to know what they had discussed. Brandeis responded that he had found Wilson "in complete sympathy with my fundamental convictions" and would support him for the presidency. Wilson in turn added that "both of us have as an object the prevention of monopoly." Then, in words new to him, Wilson went on to declare that "monopoly is created by unregulated competition, by competition that overwhelms all other competitions, and the only way to enjoy industrial freedom is to destroy that condition." In his search to restore this freedom he had called in Mr. Brandeis, who, more than anyone else he knew, had studied "corporate business from the efficiency to the political sides. I drew him out for my own thought." [9]

Brandeis came away from the interview impressed. To his brother he wrote that Wilson "is strong, simple, serious, open-minded, eager to learn, and deliberate." [10] Wilson was also impressed and a few days later translated some conference thoughts into public words. Prior to the Sea Girt meeting, Wilson had merely described the economic conditions of the United States. In his acceptance speech, the only proposal to deal with monopoly had promised a vague "rule of justice and of right," but how this could be accomplished, or what it meant, remained undefined. Moreover, Wilson had insisted that only by making corporate officials personally liable for monopolistic practices could the trust problem be solved. In Professor Link's words, "it was a totally innocuous approach to the problem." [11]

In his first speech after seeing Brandeis, Professor Wilson proved himself an apt pupil. He attacked the Rooseveltian program of regulation of monopoly and asked, "What has created these monopolies? Unregulated competition." The answer, Wilson now proposed, lay in remedial legislation to "so restrict the wrong use of competition that the right use of competition will destroy monopoly." A few days later he again attacked monopoly, this time as destructive both of economic and political freedom. At Sioux Falls, Wilson declared that "the alternative to regulating monopoly is to regulate competition." [12] But if Wilson now believed that monopoly was a result of unrestricted competition, what exactly in practical and specific terms did that mean? If he now understood the causes of the problem, what did he propose as a solution to it? On this point Wilson's speeches remained embarrassingly vague.

In late September he journeyed to Boston to speak at the Tremont Temple. Before the speech, he conferred with Brandeis, and a new note crept into his attack. "There is a point of bigness," he said, "where you pass the point of efficiency and get to the point of clumsiness and unwieldiness." Wilson here appeared inconsistent, however, since he had long maintained that he did not oppose bigness per se, only bigness attained illegally and immorally, as in a monopoly. Perhaps in an attempt to clear up his inconsistency and also to define more clearly his views *vis-à-vis* Roosevelt, Wilson telegraphed Brandeis after leaving Boston to "please set forth as explicitly as possible the actual measures by which competition can be effectively regulated. The more explicit we are on this point, the more completely will the enemies [sic] guns be spiked." [13] Brandeis

drew up a lengthy statement that not only set forth the points
that he and Wilson agreed upon but also summarized the opposing views of Roosevelt's Progressive party as seen by the
chief architect of the New Freedom:

> . . . The two parties differ fundamentally regarding the eco-
> nomic policy which the country should pursue. The Demo-
> cratic Party insists that competition can be and should be
> maintained in every branch of private industry; that competi-
> tion can be and should be restored in those branches of indus-
> try in which it has been suppressed by the trusts; and that, if
> at any future time monopoly should appear to be desirable in
> any branch of industry, the monopoly should be a public one
> —monopoly owned by the people and not by the capitalists.
> The New Party, on the other hand, insists that private mo-
> nopoly may be desirable in some branches of industry, or at
> all events, is inevitable; and that existing trusts should not be
> dismembered or forcibly dislodged from those branches of in-
> dustry in which they have already acquired a monopoly, but
> should be made "good" by regulation. In other words, the
> New Party declares that private monopoly in industry is not
> necessarily evil, but may do evil; and that legislation should
> be limited to such laws and regulations as should attempt
> merely to prevent the doing of evil. The New Party does not
> fear commercial power, however great, if only methods for reg-
> ulations are provided. We believe that no methods of regula-
> tion ever have been or can be devised to remove the menace
> inherent in private monopoly and overweening commercial
> power.[14]

In the memorandum Brandeis went on to clarify several
points, so that Wilson could remove some of the ambiguities
from his speeches. Although Wilson accepted these ideas, he
and Brandeis both agreed that it might be best if the candidate
did not state them quite so boldly. William Gibbs McAdoo
then suggested that Brandeis work up the notes into articles;
this way the proposals could be aired without Wilson incurring
any political liability. Brandeis, already under pressure from
Norman Hapgood to contribute some articles to *Collier's*, readily acquiesced and, when Wilson agreed to the plan, immediately set to work. In the next few weeks *Collier's* ran several ar-

ticles under Brandeis's signature and several other pieces appeared under the guise of editorials by Hapgood.[15]

Wilson studied the articles carefully, and at this point the two men's views really converged. The memorandum and articles posit a society grounded on a small-unit, highly competitive economy. In the past, such competition had been ruthless, leading to a survival of the fittest. But the most fit in terms of survival may not be the most fit in terms of moral needs. When America underwent the pains of economic maturation many unethical practices prevailed, and monopolies resulted from the advantages such practices bestowed. Both Brandeis and Wilson understood the connection between economic freedom and political independence. "No nation can remain free," said Wilson, "in which a small group determines the industrial development; and by determining the industrial development, determines the political policy." [16]

Like Jefferson, Jackson, and Bryan before him, Wilson stood for the small entrepreneur as against the big established businessman. Time and again he appealed for the little fellow and inveighed against the submergence of individual opportunity: "What this country needs above everything else is a body of laws which will look after the men who are on the make rather than the men who are already made"; "American enterprise is not free; the man with only a little capital is finding it harder to get into the field, more and more impossible to compete with the big fellow"; "The treasury of America ... depends upon the ... unknown man." [17] Wilson totally opposed Roosevelt's concept of the New Nationalism. Nothing could have been more repugnant to him than the Rough Rider's proposal for handling the Trusts:

> This nation should definitely adopt the policy of attacking not the mere fact of combination, but the evils and wrongdoing which so frequently accompany combination.... We should enter upon a course of supervision, control, and regulation of these great corporations—a regulation which we should not fear, if necessary, to bring to the point of control of monopoly prices.[18]

Where the New Nationalism favored economic cooperation, the New Freedom believed in competition on moral as
well as economic grounds. When Roosevelt argued for the
greater efficiency of the large unit, Wilson spoke for the democratic value of the small unit. Brandeis recognized that small
units may be wasteful at times; democracy itself is a wasteful
system, yet we cheerfully put up with these wastes for the political liberties which more than compensate for them. Brandeis
feared excessive, overefficient government as much as Roosevelt's friend Herbert Croly feared excessive individualism, to
which he countered with a governmental safeguard. This, in
part, helps to explain the Wilson-Brandeis desire for greater individual liberty under a simplistic government, while Roosevelt and Croly called for a strong social organism, superior to
the individual, in a system designed primarily for efficiency.
Carried to extremes one program could lead to anarchy, the
other to fascism.

Wilson's quandary prior to the Sea Girt meeting lay in his
failure to see any other solution than Roosevelt's, a solution he
could not accept, since he considered big government as much
an anathema as big business. The Brandeisian approach appealed to a Southerner who believed that a government governs best when it governs least. Big business, basically inefficient, was socially less desirable than small, individual
enterprise. Monopolies could be prevented by establishing
rules of competition designed to be enforced by government
with a minimum of interference into the economy and the society; the traditional role of government as protector against
transgressors would be preserved. The beauty of the Brandeisian program was that Wilson could have his cake and eat it
too—small enterprise and limited government. The problem,
as Hofstadter points out, is that "no one, not even Brandeis,
knew how to define or measure superior efficiency, or to draw a
line in the progress toward bigness, beyond which it would
lose, rather than gain, in efficiency." [19]

But size alone was not the problem: the Progressives
feared the concentration of power that bigness created and centered in just a handful of firms and indviduals. By 1899, mo-

nopolistic groups accounted for nearly one-third of the value added by industry to the gross national product. In the next fifteen years the figures grew even more alarming. The concepts of "concentration, combination, and control" dominated American industry. The debate, therefore, did involve real questions: Should the country follow the Rooseveltian doctrine of accepting the facts of large-scale monopolization and subject it to governmental regulations; or should it follow Wilson's call to reverse the trend, reestablish a basically competitive society, and regulate that competition? Had it been only a question of economic policy perhaps all the turmoil and confusion could have been avoided. Had it been only economics, perhaps it would not really have mattered which fork of the road Americans chose. But, as Louis Hartz pointed out, the trust "was just as much a psychological creation of the American Progressive mind" as it was an economic creation of American history.[20] By choosing Wilson, the voters expressed not only a choice of economic policy, but one of psychological and moral alternatives as well. As Jackson nearly a century before had rooted up and thus destroyed the Bank of the United States, so they hoped now Wilson by restoring competition could root up and destroy the trusts. It was an exercise in futility; the conditions that made the trusts possible also guaranteed their continuance. Wilson himself knew this. Despite their evils, "nobody can fail to see that modern business is going to be done by corporations. The old time of individual competition is probably gone by. . . . We will do business, henceforth, when we do it on a great and successful scale." Just prior to this statement, he had despaired of ever setting up competition among individuals but hoped perhaps competition could be established between giant corporations.[21]

In addition to the facts of economic reality, there also existed a psychological counterweight balancing the Progressives' fear of trusts. In a very real sense Americans have always judged success on a quantitative basis, with the "best" often equated with the "most." This can be traced back to the Puritan view of material success as a secular sign of spiritual salvation. To many people the size of giant corporations was indeed

awesome but simultaneously admirable, a success to be emu-
lated if possible. One of the great figures of American legend is
the Yankee merchant trader hawking his wares, shrewdly
buying and selling, growing and expanding, sending his ships
out upon all the seven seas to bring back the wares of the
world and its money to American shores and for American con-
sumption. The term "Yankee" became synonymous with shrewdness and business success, and "business" at times seemed peculiarly an American vocation. Combined with native American
ingenuity (the result of frontier necessity), American know-
how, operating through the American system of free enterprise,
harnessed the resources of this continent and gave to the citizens of this country the greatest material standard of living the
world has ever seen.

To succeed in business, especially to succeed on a large
scale, could not be condemned in America—it was too much
American, too much a part of the American success story. (And
the ultimate rationalization here was to succeed until one was
so big that a monopoly occurred.) If the methods used in this
success were not the most ethical, if they cut the line between
fraud and shrewdness a bit close, was this un-American, or just
what Frederick Jackson Turner called the unlovelier side of
another great American institution, the frontier? Yankee
shrewdness, after all, was an intrinsic part of the portrait.

Driven by the necessities of political expediency to
counter Roosevelt's New Nationalism, lured by the hope Brandeis offered, Wilson attempted the impossible: to turn back
historical progress, though he was too much the historian not
to realize the effort could end only in failure; to punish those
who had succeeded too well, though he was too much the son
of a Calvinist minister not to appreciate that material reward
which indicated spiritual salvation also. Finally, while he de-
plored bigness and monopoly, he was too proud an American
not to boast occasionally of their achievement. With his election Wilson turned to the task of reconciling these contradictions.

The New Freedom's attack on monopoly legislatively took
three forms: tariff revision, currency reform, and a strengthen-

ing of the antitrust law. Wilson chose to attack the tariff problem first because the Democratic party stood united on that issue and it seemed the best place to start. Although Brandeis had first contacted Wilson on the tariff problem, there is no evidence that he advised the President on this matter. But on currency reform and trust law Brandeis exerted a powerful, and decisive, influence. While well-informed on the tariff, Wilson knew very little about banking and finance, which may have been fortunate, since banking reform involved much more than mere economics.

Wilson had called the concentration of fiscal power in Wall Street "the most pernicious of all trusts." A gold Democrat in 1896, he had written after Bryan's defeat that "nothing but currency reform can touch the cause of the present discontent." Between 1910 and 1914, Wilson evolved two basic premises. First, a money trust of monopoly proportions existed; to restore competition it had to be destroyed. Here Brandeis's series of articles on "other people's money" confirmed Wilson's belief in the existence of a money trust; he read the articles carefully, making notes in the margins.[22] Early in 1913 the President-elect argued: "You must put the credit of this country at the disposal of everybody upon equal terms. Now, I am not entering into an indictment against the banking methods of this country. The banking system of this country does not need to be indicted. It is convicted." In his message to Congress urging reform, Wilson made the destruction of this monopoly, in order to restore competition, the major purpose of the legislation.[23]

Second, the President believed banking too important a business to be left to the bankers. Reform would make the banks what they should be—the servants, not the masters, of business. It would not be enough merely to destroy the monopoly, nor even to guarantee that it would not be re-created. Banking was so much a matter of public concern, Wilson believed, that the interests of the people must be protected via governmental supervision.

In the spring of 1913, with Wilson's blessing, Representative Carter Glass of Virginia and economist H. Parker Willis worked up a plan for a decentralized, privately controlled reserve system of not more than twenty independent reserve banks. Wilson tentatively agreed and made several suggestions, the most important an "altruistic Federal Reserve Board in Washington to supervise the proposed system," a "capstone" to it. Glass did not like the idea but acquiesced. In general the Glass-Willis plan was cautious and conservative, aimed at winning the support of a broad spectrum of respectable business and banking leaders, with control of the system and of currency in private hands.

The plan immediately aroused the antagonism of the Populist wing of the Democratic party. William Jennings Bryan and his followers had two main points of contention. First, the Glass proposal allowed bankers to elect members of the Federal Reserve Board; and second, currency issue remained in bank control. He wanted the Board composed solely of government-appointed officials, and more importantly, he wanted note issue to be solely a governmental function. He informed Wilson that the Democracy since Jefferson and Jackson—as well as in recent platforms—had believed in currency issue as a governmental function. As the bill stood, he regretfully informed the President, he could not support it and could not ask his followers to do so either.[24]

Wilson's dislike of governmental control and centralization had led him originally to support the Glass bill, which as Bryan realized was nothing more than a decentralized private system. Senator Robert Owen also saw this and sent Wilson copies of recent Democratic planks on the currency question, planks which of course echoed the Bryanite view.[25] At stake basically was the nature of the banking system. On the one hand Glass proposed an essentially private, decentralized scheme with just a modicum of government control. The more progressive wing of the party demanded outright governmental control, realizing that if the currency power remained under banker control and banker representatives composed the Federal Reserve Board, then the money trust would not be broken up but merely reorganized with more power than before and given government sanction.

In early June, Wilson had to decide between the conservative Glass-Parker bill, which would have banker support, and the main points of the Bryan group. So on June 11, 1913, he called in one of the few men whose economic views he trusted and respected—Louis Brandeis. The Boston lawyer distrusted the big banking houses almost to the point of obsession. He had once said that

> We have no place in American democracy for the money king, not even for the merchant prince. We are confronted in the twentieth century, as we were in the nineteenth century, with an irreconcilable conflict. Our democracy cannot endure half free and half slave. The essence of the trust is a combination of the capitalist, by the capitalist, and for the capitalist.[26]

Brandeis convinced the President not only of the justness of William Jennings Bryan's arguments in light of Democratic platform pledges but also of their rightness. Even if the backing of Federal Reserve notes should be commercial paper, the currency must be exclusively a function of the government. As for banker control, "the American people will not be content to have the discretion necessarily involved vested in a Board composed wholly or in part of bankers; for their judgment may be biased by private interests or affiliations." To bolster these views, Brandeis sounded a dire note on the conflict "between the policies of the Administration and the desires of the financiers and of big business," a conflict he termed "irreconcilable" and in which concessions, in the end, would prove futile.[27]

On June 18, Wilson summoned Secretary of the Treasury William Gibbs McAdoo, Glass, and Owen to the White House and informed them that he had decided to insist upon exclusive government control of the Reserve System and on making its notes government obligations. Bryan was ecstatic and in a public letter declared it a bill "written from the standpoint of the people rather than from the standpoint of the financiers." The government issue provisions, he said, fulfilled Democratic platform principles. With Glass and the Bryanites reconciled, the President proposed the bill to Congress on June 23 and despite strong attacks from the banking community, engineered it through Congress and signed it into law before the year ended.

In retrospect, it stands as the single most constructive piece of legislation enacted in the Wilson Administration, and one of the most important in the history of the country.

Imperfect in many details, it nevertheless struck that careful balance between private control and public supervision that Wilson and Brandeis so idealized. In a very short time it won the approval of the bankers, especially of the smaller country banks now released from liege to Wall Street.[28] The extreme radicals, however, condemned it. LaFollette denounced it as a "big bankers' bill" legalizing the money trust.[29] Senator Joseph H. Bristow of Kansas and Representative Charles A. Lindbergh of Minnesota echoed this charge; in their criticism, they failed to understand the nature of Wilsonian reform.

The New Freedom, basically conservative, looked not to reform and redo society in a new mode but to return to an idyllic (and perhaps semimythical) past in which the various political and economic groups of the country had existed in near-perfect harmony. To the extent that it favored popular democracy against a status quo favoring a wealthy élite, it was progressive, but it also demanded minimal governmental regulation. This partially explains Wilson's dilemma regarding big business—how to combat it without utilizing big government. The Brandeisian approach of using government to establish and then regulate a competitive condition rather than regulating business apparently solved the President's anguish. Both Wilson and Brandeis feared letting the government go too far. The Bryanites, some of whom favored a government-owned and operated system, failed to understand that for the President and his advisor, the proposed cure was worse than the ill. In essence, their plan ran along the Rooseveltian lines of substituting big government for big business. In the long run, big government came, and it is ironic that under Wilson this country first experienced both the benefits and the disadvantages of Leviathan. But in December 1913, looking over their handiwork, both men were satisfied that they had struck their sought-for balance.[30]

When it became clear that the Federal Reserve bill would be passed, Wilson and his Administration turned to the prob-

lem of what legislation to propose next. Several members of the
Cabinet urged the President to do nothing more; business
should be given the chance to adjust to the new currency and
tariff laws. Secretary of Agriculture David Houston advised
Wilson "to make haste slowly." Albert S. Burleson, Lindley M.
Garrison, and James C. McReynolds all argued against any new
business legislation. In New York the banking community
braced for adoption of the new reserve system, dreading any
trust measure in which Brandeis would have a voice. And from
Boston came advice from Henry Lee Higginson, who pleaded
with the President to forego any new legislation which could
affect industry and commerce.[31]

But William Jennings Bryan urged Wilson to go on and
to fulfill the Democratic pledges on the trusts. From Boston
also came advice from Louis Brandeis—*Be Bold!* Not only was
antitrust legislation essential to fulfilling the New Freedom but
also to "politically satisfy the demands of the very large number of progressive Democrats and the near Democrats who are
already beginning to express some doubts" regarding the Administration's courage. The so-called business depression "cannot be ended or lessened by any course which the administration may take. . . . The fearless course is the wise one." [32]
Wilson, beset by such conflicting views, mulled the problem
over during his Christmas vacation.

Wilson's views on the subject were fairly clear, straightfor-
ward, and naïve: prevent monopoly by punishment of personal
guilt. If men were punished for their sins and these sins exposed to public condemnation, then they would sin no more.
This was simple enough to say, but how to do it? Wilson certainly did not know, and, except for a strong enforcement of the
Sherman Act's criminal provisions, he never set forth any
clear-cut program. Moreover, he was not even sure that the
trusts could be broken up. Several times he had stated his belief that big business was here to stay, but he also averred "that
real dissolution in the case of the trusts is the only thing we
can rest satisfied with." [33] Wilson's problem again reflected his
basic ambivalence: fear of both big business and of big government.

If Wilson approached the trust problem in the role of po-

litical moralist, his most trusted advisor came in the garb of social and economic moralist; but Brandeis's morality was
tempered by a pragmatism regarding the differences between
how men should act and how they did act. Brandeis leaned toward Adam Smith's view of the basically greedy nature of economic man. Before Congressional hearings on trust legislation
he had maintained that antitrust measures would never be
effectively enforced through criminal proceedings alone. To
another committee he had said he saw no hope that searing the
monopolists "alleged consciences" would produce any results at
all. The proper method would be to decide on the desired
goals and then frame just laws which reasonable men would
follow. Over twenty years before he met Woodrow Wilson,
Brandeis had argued that "no regulation can be enforced which
is not reasonable." [34]

If both Wilson and Brandeis desired the destruction of the
trusts, their reasons often varied. Both argued that democracy
could not continue if the economic fate of the nation rested in
the hands of oligopoly. Wilson's declaration that America
could have no freedom if she lacked economic liberty neatly
answered Brandeis's question, "Shall unlimited concentration of
commercial power be encouraged in a country dedicated to
equality of opportunity?" Brandeis, just as interested as the
President in keeping open the doors of opportunity to a rising
middle class, went further in his determination to save even
the wealthy from their own folly. "It is certain," he once said,
"that among a free people every excess of capital must in time
be repaid by the excessive demands of those who have not the
capital." Therefore it would be to the advantage of the capital-
ists to set up reasonable limits and end injustices.[35]

To Brandeis a trust constituted more than just a political
danger; its very size menaced the actual framework of society.
Where Wilson argued that bigness in and of itself was not bad,
only its abuses, Brandeis saw bigness itself the major threat.[36]
Here is the theme that never varied in Louis Brandeis's
thought—the curse of bigness; too great a concentration of economic power constituted a social, economic, and political menace to a free society; a business could be efficient only up to a

certain size; beyond this size bigness caused inefficiency; trusts could never stand up to smaller units in a free and truly competitive market place; proper rules regulating competition could insure such conditions; competition is the atmosphere which a free society breathes.

As Wilson contemplated the problem it is almost certain that his thoughts returned to the original memorandum Brandeis had prepared in 1912. There and in several articles the People's Attorney spelled out a four-point program to deal with the trusts: first, remove the uncertainties and vagaries of the Sherman Act; second, facilitate the enforcement of the law by the courts; next, create a board or commission to aid in administering the law; finally, allow trade agreements, subject to the commission's review, to stand if they were good and not in violation of competitive rules and void them otherwise.[37]

On January 20, 1914, Wilson delivered a special message to Congress on the "great question" of trusts and monopolies. In moderate terms, he suggested that "the antagonism between business and government is over," and the time ripe to proceed with a sensible program—a program representing "the best business judgment in America." He proposed: outlawing interlocking directorates in great corporations; allowing the Interstate Commerce Commission power to supervise capital financing and securities issuance by the railroads; creating a federal commission to provide businessmen with "the advice, the definite guidance, and information" which they need, but not having the power to "make terms with monopoly or . . . assume control of business"; establishing penalties for individuals guilty of malpractices; and providing that any facts or judgments decided upon on government suits would not have to be reproven in suits by private individuals to recover damages.[38] On reading the speech over, Louis Brandeis could well comment with satisfaction that the President "has paved the way for about all I have asked for and some of the provisions specifically are what I got into his mind at my first interview."[39]

In practical details the Administration sponsored three bills. First, the so-called Clayton bill, drawn primarily by Henry D. Clayton, chairman of the House Judiciary Commit-

tee, enumerated and outlawed various practices, including
price-cutting to destroy competition; tying clauses; the purchase of stock by one firm from another to limit competition;
provisions for criminal prosecution; fines and/or imprison-
ment for individuals guilty of illegal practices. It also outlawed
interlocking directorates and gave private individuals suing for
damages under the Sherman Act the benefit of any judgments
in government cases. A second measure created an Interstate
Trade Commission to interpret the federal laws to businessmen
and to provide expert advice and information. Known as the
Covington bill, in its original form it merely provided for an
expanded Bureau of Corporations, not the Rooseveltian ideal
of a power regulatory agency. Wilson described it as a "safe and
sensible" measure and not a dangerous experiment. The final
part of the program, the Rayburn bill, gave the Interstate
Commerce Commission power over railroad securities.

For the next few months Brandeis found himself frantically busy in Washington, tied up both in the Interstate Commerce Commission's hearings on railroad rates and in trying to
get the President's antitrust program strengthened and enacted.
The more radical Progressives were disappointed by Wilson's
message and hoped that the program would be modified before passage. Samuel Untermyer complained to Colonel House
that the proposed bills were "lamentably weak and ineffective
... [the] so-called Trade Commission Bill is nothing more at
present than a Bureau of Information with little more than the
existing Bureau of Corporations and with vastly added ex-
pense." He begged House to get Brandeis in to redraw the
measure. House evidently agreed and when he forwarded Untermyer's letter to the President he urged him "to put Gregory
and Brandeis on this job with the Attorney-General to act as
advisor." [40] Wilson took up the suggestion with alacrity, writing to Congressman William C. Adamson that Brandeis was in
Washington and urging him to have Brandeis appear before
the House Committee that was holding hearings on the Clayton and Trade Commission bills. Francis Newlands also contacted Brandeis, requesting his views on the proposed measures. Brandeis reluctantly agreed, although he much preferred

to continue the intricate work on the I.C.C. hearings. For several days in mid-February he testified before the House Judiciary Committee.[41]

Brandeis was not altogether happy with the details of the proposed measure and on February 22 sent Attorney-General James C. McReynolds a long detailed letter suggesting ways of strengthening the antitrust law. McReynolds, probably acting upon Wilson's suggestion, earlier had requested Brandeis's views. The Boston lawyer particularly wanted the section dealing with interlocking directorates made foolproof. He had urged the House committee to realize the importance of this idea and lectured them on the dangers: "the principle that no man can serve two masters . . . is fundamental, and when a man undertakes to serve two corporations that are dealing with one another there is always the danger that the unethical relation may result in loss . . . generally to the public through lessened efficiency." [42] He reminded McReynolds that the prohibition against interlocking directorates had been omitted from the money bill on the pledge that it would be included in antitrust legislation, and that such a clause would "stop the concentration of money power." On March 1, he closeted himself with the Attorney-General and his advisors for the better part of the day going over all the parts of the program. Two weeks later Congressman Clayton agreed to the insertion of a strong prohibition and requested Brandeis to send him the measure.[43] On June 5, a weak Trade Commission bill, together with the Clayton and Rayburn bills, passed the House of Representatives. But once the bills reached the Senate, pressures built up to change them, pressures based on the belief that the bills were unrealistic, ineffective, and totally unworkable.

The provision on individual guilt, so dear to Wilson's heart, scared both large and small businessmen. After the mad scramble of unrestrained and cutthroat competition of the Gilded Age, American businessmen began to look for methods that would avoid not only such destructive excesses but also avoid governmental regulation. The details for the great trade association activities of the 1920s were being worked out at this time, and the Clayton bill threatened to halt this "new cooperation." Conceivably, a zealot in the Attorney-General's office could interpret the law so as to reward any act of cooperation with a fine and/or jail sentence. In addition, a widespread belief existed that denied the possibility of statutorily defining all practices in restraint of trade. Brandeis had himself admitted the great difficulty of trying to define in advance all illicit methods of competition.[44] George Rublee later recalled the fears that in attempting to be too specific, the Clayton Act would leave open the doors to every sort of evasion that could be developed by American ingenuity.[45] Most critics of the program came to the conclusion that a strong trade commission, with discretionary powers, should enforce the legislative wishes as defined in general but comprehensive terms. Rather than attempt to define all illegal practices, they argued, outlaw all such practices in general terms and let the commission decide upon specifics. Wilson, upset and confused by the criticism, nonetheless realized the validity of the arguments. But he hesitated, his old fears against governmental regulation still strong.

At this point, Brandeis acted decisively to alter the President's thinking. George Rublee and Congressman Raymond B. Stevens of New Hampshire both believed in a strong Trade Commission and drew up the so-called Stevens bills, incorporating this idea as an amendment to the Covington bill. Brandeis himself, during the winter and spring of 1914, had given only cursory thought to the problem because of the I.C.C. railroad investigation. As a result, Rublee did much of the actual drafting. Both Stevens and Rublee thought that Brandeis opposed the type of commission they wanted and hesitated to discuss the matter with him. Finally, however, they got Senator Henry Hollis to make an appointment for them with the President on June 10, and Rublee asked Brandeis to go along. Rublee said he knew that Brandeis did not approve of their ideas, but if he went with them the President at least would listen to their proposals seriously. Brandeis agreed to come, and after Rublee made the presentation the President asked the Boston lawyer what he thought. Brandeis then turned on all his persuasive charm and much to everyone's surprise proceeded to tell the President why he should support the proposal. Wilson, who had already seen the Stevens bill, by this time needed only the assurances that he was not surrendering any of the New Freedom principles. Such assurance Brandeis provided.[46]

Brandeis, like Wilson, originally had opposed a Commission that smacked so much of Roosevelt's New Nationalism. But Brandeis gradually came to believe that it would be impossible to define statutorily all possible violations and that it would be better to lay down legislative guidelines which could then be expanded by a regulatory agency. Due to the I.C.C. pressures, he had neglected the Covington bill and merely awaited an opportune moment to discuss the situation with the President. Wilson now sent Brandeis to see several senators to apprise them of the situation. Brandeis himself appeared before the Senate Interstate Commerce Committee later in the month. In answer to a direct question on the Stevens' bill's parentage, he admitted that he, Rublee, and Stevens had worked it up into the final form.

Ultimately, with the aid of White House pressure, the strengthened Covington-Stevens bill passed, but several parts of the Clayton bill were toned down. By this time, however, the Progressives' attention had begun to shift away from the crusade against the trusts to the drama of the World War. Upon the United States' entry into the war, effective execution of antitrust measures ceased and would not begin again until the rise in power of the neo-Brandeisians in the second New Deal in the thirties.

The relations between Wilson and Brandeis indicated more than the obvious fact that the President relied heavily on Brandeis's advice regarding banking and antitrust reforms. Wilson, like many progressives, had a clearer idea of what troubled him than of how to solve those problems. Brandeis presented him with a possible program, but the President never carried it through to completion because at bottom, he did not understand it. Even conceding the enormous political pressures and crosscurrents with which Wilson had to deal, he demonstrated on several occasions that he did not comprehend the Brandeisian philosophy. Bigness seemed to attract him as much as monopoly repelled him, while to Brandeis they were but two facets of the same danger. We remember the New Freedom primarily for its awareness of industrial dislocations and its yearnings for an open, competitive society. The basic question is whether, even if Wilson had been more comprehending and astute, the New Freedom, as Wilson and Brandeis conceived it, had any real chances of success.

Chapter V

THE PROGRESSIVE
AS ZIONIST

In August 1914, Louis Brandeis assumed the chairmanship of the Provisional Executive Committee for Zionist Affairs, an emergency *ad hoc* organization called into being to alleviate the distress of Jews in war-torn countries of Europe and the Middle East. In the next seven years, he built up the near-moribund American Zionist organization to a position of dominance in the world movement, raised millions of dollars for the relief of war-afflicted Jews, effectively influenced the Wilson Administration to support the Balfour and San Remo declarations establishing a Jewish homeland in Palestine, and was offered the leadership of the World Zionist Organization. Yet in 1921, after a struggle with Dr. Chaim Weizmann over a seemingly minor matter, Brandeis withdrew from Zionist affairs when his followers in the Zionist Organization of America repudiated his leadership.

It is not my purpose here to explore the convolutions of Zionist politics in the years during and after World War I. Rather, I would like to advance the following hypothesis: that Brandeisian Zionism can only be understood in the light of the Progressive American reform politics with which Brandeis was associated, and that the split between Brandeis and Weizmann resulted not from a dispute over the establishment of a land-purchase fund (*Keren Ha-yesod*), but from two different and to a degree conflicting philosophies regarding Zionism and the establishment of Palestine as a Jewish homeland.[1]

Prior to 1914, American Jews as a whole showed little interest in Zionism. While orthodox Jews more or less accepted Zionism if carefully distinguished from Messianism, Reform Jews, heirs mainly of the earlier German migration, regarded Zionism as inimical to the spirit of Americanism. The leading organ of Reform Judaism had consistently denounced "the whole question of a Jewish State as foreign to the spirit of the modern Jew in this land, who looks upon America as his Palestine." Rabbi David Phillipson of Cincinnati had unequivocally declared, "The United States is our Palestine, and Washington our Jerusalem." [2] The two leading Reform organizations, the Central Conference of American Rabbis and the Union of American Hebrew Congregations, had persistently opposed Zionism.[3] Theodore Herzl's appeal to American Jews " [not to] forget in their own happiness in the glorious land of freedom, how heavy is the bondage of their brethren" went unanswered.[4]

The reason for this antipathy is fairly plain. The United States, with its melting pot mythology, emphasized allegiance, not to a foreign country or ideology, but to the American dream of equality and opportunity. Of those who had accepted this creed, many had prospered and had been allowed to live in peace; those who did not, like the Irish, many of whom persisted in their attachment to Rome, had been discriminated against. For the Jew especially, after centuries of persecution, America indeed seemed to be a Promised Land. The leading lay spokesmen for the various Jewish communities were successful and assimilated, and wanted nothing to do with a movement that, to them, smacked of the Eastern European ghettos. "We have fought our way through to liberty, equality, and fraternity," said Henry Morgenthau, Sr. "No one shall rob us of these gains. . . . We Jews of America have found America to be our Zion. Therefore I refuse to allow myself to be called a Zionist. I am an American." [5]

The dream of restoration in the Holy Land was thus to

many a pernicious chimera. The financier Jacob Schiff, a recognized lay leader of American Jews, put it bluntly when he refused to meet with Herzl: "If he wishes to discuss Zionism [I] am unwilling to do so as with deepest attachment to my brethren in faith and race, I am an American pure and simple, and cannot possibly belong to two nations. I feel that Zionism is a purely theoretical and sentimental proposition and as a practicable one has no future." [6] What centuries of persecution had been unable to do—erase that mystical attachment of the Jew to the land of Israel—opportunity and tolerance in a frontier society was now accomplishing. Despite an upsurge in anti-Semitism that accompanied the great influx of Jews from Eastern Europe after 1880, the United States still remained the most tolerant land in the world as far as Jews were concerned, and the dominant Jewish community in the United States looked not to restoration in Palestine, but to assimilation in America.[7]

As long as the Zionist ideology postulated, however subtly, that all Jews should go to Palestine, it ran counter not only to the prevailing hope for assimilation among Reform elements, but also to the demands of the United States that immigrants to these shores become Americans and forego any other loyalties. The success of Zionism in this country would depend, therefore, upon the ability of its leaders to find a form that would not clash with Americanism, and a role so unique that only Americans could perform it. For this task, Louis Brandeis was ideally qualified.

From all reports, Brandeis's contacts with Judaism before 1910 were very tenuous. His family, except for an uncle, were freethinkers, and his brother-in-law, Felix Adler, had founded the quasi-religious Ethical Culture Society. "My early training was not Jewish in a religious sense, nor was it Christian," Brandeis said. "While naturally interested in their race, my people were not so narrow as to allow their religious belief to overshadow their interest in the broader aspects of humanity." [8]

Brandeis's years in Boston contributed little to any nascent sense of Jewish identity he may have had. The prevailing mode of Jewish thought in that city in the late nineteenth century reflected the assimilationist beliefs of Rabbi Solomon Schindler, head of the Reform Temple Israel. Schindler spoke on behalf of those Jews who had found a place in Boston, and who had been more or less accepted by the Brahmin leadership. His sermons on modern Judaism were heavily attended by both Gentiles and Jews, and reprinted in both book form and newspaper serialization.

Schindler had little use for Zionism, or for Messianism of any sort. Jewish emancipation following the French and American revolutions had eliminated the need for radical change in the situation of the Jews; in a free country like the United States, assimilation was a far more attractive prospect than restoration to Palestine. Here Jews enjoyed each and every political right and freedom that any other person did. Why return with some leader to a poverty-stricken desert on the Mediterranean, where the leader would probably want to rule by himself? The *Boston Transcript,* commenting on Schindler's views, happily noted that Jews did not wish to leave Boston for Palestine, and had thus proved that they were "as American as any of us can be." [9]

Although he never belonged to any synagogue or temple, Brandeis did contribute to a number of Jewish charities. He was a charter subscriber to the Federation of Jewish Charities in Boston in 1895, and supported the Hebrew Industrial School. In 1903, he gave one of the dedication speeches at the opening of the enlarged Mt. Sinai Hospital on Staniford Street.[10] Yet even here there is no real identification as a Jew; he gave as generously to a number of non-Jewish charities, and donated even more to the various public service groups with which he affiliated. Among the lists of those with whom he associated in Boston reforms, there were few Jewish names. When it came to promoting savings bank life insurance, he had to call on a young law student to be sure that various Jewish groups knew the importance of the reform.[11]

Though extremely well read he had a curious gap in his knowledge of things religious; his speeches and letters were dotted with quotations from the great secular works of literature, but rarely from the Bible, and then usually from the New Testament.[12] Supposedly in August, 1897, he had read of

Theodore Herzl's address to the first Zionist Congress and had commented to his wife, "There is a cause to which I could give my life." [13] Yet he did not become a Zionist for another fifteen years. "During most of my life," he said in 1915, "my contact with Jews and Judaism was slight. I gave little thought to their problems, save in asking myself, from time to time, whether we were showing by our lives due appreciation of the opportunities which this hospitable country affords." [14] He had for many years firmly believed in assimilation, and anticipated Theodore Roosevelt's denunciation of so-called hyphenated Americans with dual loyalties.[15]

In 1910, two events launched the conversion of Louis Brandeis to Zionism. First, he met Jacob deHaas, former secretary to the great Herzl. deHaas, while interviewing him for the *Jewish Advocate* about savings bank life insurance, asked him if he were related to Lewis Naphtali Dembitz. When Brandeis said that Dembitz was his uncle, deHaas noted that he had also been a "noble Jew." Brandeis asked deHaas to explain, and for the next two hours listened while stories of Herzl and the Zionist movement poured forth from the young writer. Over the next several months, the two men met frequently, and Brandeis, as was his custom, began to read voraciously.[16]

If deHaas stimulated him intellectually, the second event moved him emotionally. At the behest of his friend and client, A. Lincoln Filene, Brandeis had been invited to mediate between garment manufacturers and the clothing workers' unions in the New York strike. Brandeis had, until this time, known mainly the upper-class Jews of German origin; now, for the first time, he came into contact with the masses of East European Jewry. Their idealism fired his imagination. Compared to the paternalistic labor relations that characterized the New England mills, the garment industry was a living model of democracy. Workers and bosses shouted at one another in Yiddish, and on one occasion he heard a shop operator denounce his employer with a quotation from Isaiah:

> It is you who have devoured the vineyard, the spoil of the poor, is in your houses.

What do you mean by crushing My people, by grinding the
face of the poor? says the Lord God of hosts.[17]

By 1912 he had formally joined the Zionists, although the
report of his affiliation created no excitement at that year's convention. Then, in 1913, he surprised even his family when he
took the platform to introduce Nahum Sokolow to Boston. Sokolow, a leading European Zionist, was greatly impressed by
Brandeis, and in his report to the Zionist Congress of that year
made his meeting with Brandeis the leading theme of his
American visit.[18] By this time, Brandeis's name had become
more familiar to American Jewish leaders who, although they
appreciated his interest in the movement, were still put off by
his un-Jewishness. When war broke out in Europe in the summer of 1914, the various factions of the American Zionists gathered in New York to plan aid to their European brethren.
Brandeis's national reputation, his influence with the Wilson
Administration, his continued interest in Zionism, and his neu-
trality in internecine feuds made him a natural choice to head
the emergency Provisional Committee.

In accepting the chairmanship, Brandeis explained what
had drawn him to the movement: "I find Jews possessed of
those very qualities which we of the twentieth century seek to
develop in our struggle for justice and democracy—a deep
moral feeling which makes them capable of noble acts; a deep
sense of the brotherhood of man; and a high intelligence, the
fruit of three thousand years of civilization." [19] He later noted
the tone that would affect his entire leadership of the Zionists:
"My approach to Zionism was through Americanism. In time
practical experience and observation convinced me that Jews
were by reason of their traditions and their character peculiarly
fitted for the attainment of American ideals. Gradually it became clear to me that to be good Americans, we must be better
Jews, and to be better Jews, we must become Zionists." [20]

What he failed to add was that the American ideals he admired were of a certain type—the Jeffersonian belief in a society founded upon a small-unit economy; the state serving
only to insure that no man would injure his neighbor and, in

some cases, protecting the helpless and the weak; a frontier faith in cooperation among men; an openness and generosity among people devoted to common goals. As Louis Levinthal pointed out, "Brandeis saw in Zionism the means of realizing in Palestine more quickly and more completely those social ideals that America has striven, and is still striving, to make real." [21] The limited size of Palestine, which others saw as a handicap to progress, Brandeis viewed as a blessing. There would be no "curse of bigness" there, no vested interests, but room for opportunity and social experimentation.[22] Like many Progressives, Brandeis believed in the possibilities of applying science to human affairs through social engineering, and Palestine could provide the laboratory in which a controlled experiment could take place.

I do not wish to imply that Brandeis came to be a Zionist only because he thought the movement would allow him an opportunity to do what he had been unable to accomplish through his American reforms. He admired Jewish ideals and sympathized with the goals of the Zionists. All of these traits, it should be noted, are secular, however, the qualities of mind and labor; Brandeis accepted the ethics of Judaism, but not its piety. Only his belief that a Jewish homeland would allow Jews there to be free to be different made any recognition of the distinct religious nature of Judaism.

Brandeis became a Zionist for a variety of reasons, of which his Progressive experience and ideals were most important. There was also, however, his detestation of any form of prejudice. While I would not agree with Ben-Gurion's claim that Brandeis became a Zionist only because of the injustice he saw,[23] I would certainly agree that it made a great deal of difference in his support of the movement.

Recently, some revisionist historians have argued that the prime motivation of Brandeis's conversion to Zionism was his hunger for political advancement. Yonathan Shapiro suggests that Brandeis turned to Zionism only after his first "bid for power—when he was considered by President Wilson for a Cabinet post—failed, owing to strong opposition, which included that of powerful Jewish businessmen." Shapiro bases his contention on such "facts" that Brandeis did not become a Zionist until he had failed in his Cabinet "bid," that Brandeis wrote letters to his brother in which the political aspects of his Zionism were noted, that Brandeis then cultivated Jewish leaders in order to have their support in his second bid (the Supreme Court nomination), and that Wilson invited Jewish support in 1916 by naming Brandeis to the Court.[24] Shapiro moreover notes the suddenness of Brandeis's conversion and reads political opportunism into this.

This is a serious misreading of the nature both of the relationship between Brandeis and Wilson and of Brandeisian Zionism. Because Brandeis opposed politics based upon ethnic origins does not mean that he changed his mind when he became a Zionist. Part of the appeal he had to other American Jews was his establishing a Zionism that allowed them to be both Americans and Zionists; that he recognized the political nuances of Zionism does not prove opportunism, but merely political sophistication. Part of his effectiveness, after all, was his ability to influence people in power, a trait he had developed in Puritan Massachusetts long before he became a Zionist.

Brandeis was shut out of the Cabinet in 1913 not because of Jewish opposition, but because of Democratic opposition, especially from Boston, where he had antagonized the local machinery. Wilson, trying to maintain party unity after his election, could not afford to antagonize the party chieftains, who had been much more important in his victory than had been the so-called Jewish vote. Wilson called on Brandeis continuously between 1913 and 1916 to advise him on a number of issues and had determined to reward him when the proper moment came.[25]

Wilson's nomination of Brandeis to the high bench in 1916 served at least two purposes: it rewarded and honored Brandeis for the services he had rendered to the President, and it appealed to certain groups in the electorate whose support Wilson would need in order to be reelected in 1916. The question is, which group or groups did Wilson hope to influence. Shapiro argues that Wilson wanted to gain the support of the Jewish voters, and that both he and Brandeis thus capitalized on the latter's Zionist alignment. The difficulties with this hypothesis is that it fails to note that the so-called Jewish vote was negligible outside of a few northeastern cities, and even there it had not yet become the swing vote it would in the 1930s. Moreover, the danger of an anti-Semitic backlash far outweighed any benefit from a few Jewish votes. If Wilson was banking on Brandeis in order to win the election by the Jewish vote, then he was indeed a poor politician.

Brandeis's appointment certainly was designed in part to win votes, but not just from the Jews. Wilson in 1912 had won, but only by a plurality of a little over 40 percent. In order to win in 1916, he had to attract the different progressive alliances that had supported Theodore Roosevelt in 1912. Here Brandeis was a key figure, since he held the respect of many of the leading Roosevelt backers, as well as those who followed Wisconsin's Robert M. LaFollette. The social justice advocates, the champions of wage and hours laws, the defenders of children, the promoters of scientific management and conservation—to all of them Brandeis was a Progressive of Progressives.

The important point of his Zionism is that he carried out his leadership in the best of progressive traditions, capitalizing on all he had learned in previous battles. In sum, *Zionism was a reform*. Brandeis studied the data, organized his followers, decided not only on an ideal solution, but also on one that could be practicably achieved, and then he set out to achieve it. During the years that he headed the American Zionists, Brandeis acted just as he had when he had led his backers to defeat the New Haven merger or to push through savings bank life insurance. He brought to bear not only the same outlook, but adopted essentially the same tactics. His motto, constantly repeated, was "Money. Members. Discipline." [26] In August, 1914, there were 12,000 enrolled members in the Federation of American Zionists; by the 1919 convention, membership lists totaled 177,000. From an annual budget of $12,150, Brandeis expanded Zionist activities into enterprises involving millions.[27] Aided by his friendship with Wilson and other important members of the Administration, he managed to enlist the government's help for Zionist efforts to relieve war distress.

The Balfour Declaration and San Remo convention were due in part to his efforts.

The detailing of the accomplishments of the Provisional Committee must be reserved for another account, but the point I wish to emphasize here is how akin Brandeis's Zionist efforts were to his earlier achievements in different political reforms. He concentrated on practical details, to the extent that by 1916 European-oriented members of the American movement complained that "too little time was devoted to theoretical reviews and academic formulations of policy" because the leadership was "too practical, too much concerned with practical plans." [28] He emphasized the need for a widespread and democratic participation in the movement, much to the chagrin of the aristocratic leaders who had dominated American Jewry up to that time.[29] Finally, he gave generously both of his time and his money.[30]

Brandeis thus accomplished what was necessary: he made Zionism respectable for American Jews. He quieted the fears of the assimilationists by emphasizing that Palestine was an option, not a necessity. "No Jews will be *sent* to Palestine," he explained. "The place is made ready; legal right of habitation is secured; and any who wish are free to go. But it is of the essence of Zionism that there shall be no compulsion." [31] By providing America with the task of financier to the world movement, he gave it the unique role it was seeking. In Americanizing Zionism, however, he of necessity brought himself and his followers into conflict with the European tradition and ethos, as personified by Chaim Weizmann.

Shmaryahu Levin once noted that for East European Jews, Zionism was a matter of course. In countries where Jewish masses were subject to constant pressures, their national consciousness, in order to survive, had turned to Zionism.[32] So it was with Chaim Weizmann. From the time of his youth in a small *shtetl* in Russia, through all his years in England, to his death as president of the nation he had done so much to create, Weizmann's energies concentrated on Zionism. But just as Brandeis's Zionism grew out of and reflected the nature of American reform, so that of Weizmann arose from the East Europe which had produced him. Cosmopolitan, with irresistible charm and a brilliant scientific mind, Weizmann never really left the intellectual environment of the *Ostjuden*.[33]

Weizmann first came to prominence as a member of a group opposing Theodore Herzl. With fellow students from Eastern Europe, including Martin Buber, Weizmann formed the so-called "Democratic Fraction," which opposed the established Zionist leaders like Herzl, Max Nordau, Leopold Greenburg, and Max Mandelstamm. For Weizmann, the Westerners stood too far away from the true heart of Zion, the Russian-Jewish masses.[34] After the death of Herzl, they succeeded in leading the Zionist movement away from emphasis on political action toward a renewal of cultural awareness and a belief in colonization.

The most articulate spokesman for this view was Asher Ginzberg, who wrote under the pseudonym of Achad Ha'am, "A Man of the People." Ginzberg's writings strove toward a conceptualization of the Jew as a member of a spiritual community; Zionism, therefore, had to start with the basis of Jewish cultural and national consciousness, and the only true leaders of Zion could be those who were in tune with the masses. Western Jews, by their very nature and as a result of the social milieu in which they lived, were incapable of being real Jewish leaders. Western nations had shifted the moral problem from Judaism to Jews, that is, from the nation to the individual. In their democracy, they had made possible the emancipation of the Jew as an individual, but in so doing had cut out the national consciousness. Achad Ha'am might have been anticipating Brandeis when he wrote in 1897: "Almost all our great men, those, that is, whose education and social position fit them to be at the head of a Jewish State, are spiritually far removed from Judaism, and have no true conception of its nature and its value. Such men, however loyal to their State and devoted to its interests, will necessarily regard those interests as bound up with the foreign culture which they themselves have imbibed; and they will endeavor, by moral suasion or even by force, to implant that culture in the Jewish State." [35] Like Ginzberg, Weizmann never really trusted those who did not come from the East. "For assimilated Jews," he wrote, referring to all Westerners, Judaism "was a sealed book; in their complete alienation from the masses, the source of inspiration, they had not the slightest concept of the inner significance, the constructive moral-ethical-social character of Zionism." [36]

For Weizmann and his followers, a Jewish homeland had to be a fixed center of spiritual values, a veritable throbbing, pulsating heart of Judaism itself.[37] Given the conditions of the Russian Pale—the Hasidic mysticism, the persecution, the superstition, and the messianic hopes—it was but a short and obvious step to connect Herzl's political Zionism with the age-old dream of returning to Jerusalem with the messiah. The more sophisticated leaders, of course, never assumed that connection, but implicitly the call of Zionism raised again messianic hopes. Weizmann never claimed to be a messiah, but he inspired an intense devotion among his followers, and in time came to share much of their belief in restoration.[38]

Zionism to Weizmann appeared as a mission, involving the highest of principles, and on the subject he was fanatical. Felix Frankfurter recalled that, despite his learning, nothing else except Palestine interested Weizmann. He would respond to anything involving Zionism and ignored everything else. "The whole of his life became for him a function of the realization of the reclamation, the rehabilitation, the investiture of Palestine by the Jewish people. . . . Most people scatter their energies, or enfeeble them, or say 'Yes, but. . . ,'—well, there were no buts in Weizmann's makeup." [39] Zionism took up all of Weizmann's life, and he found it impossible to understand anyone who viewed the movement in another way. He gloried in the endless European debates over the fine points of theory, and came to grips with facts only when necessary, if at all.[40]

Here, then, was the basic conflict between Louis Brandeis and Chaim Weizmann. The one saw Zionism coolly, intellectually, in terms of a job that could be done; the other emotionally, fervidly, dedicated to a mission. Each was almost archetypically the result of his environment, and the characterization of the feud between them was aptly labeled "Washington versus Pinsk." The temperament of the two types of Zionism reflected in the two men and their followers all too frequently made it a case of personality rather than of outlook. Both wanted the same thing and went about getting it different ways; both were absolutely essential to the ultimate success of Zionism; and both were absolutely incapable of preventing the difficulties that arose between them.

Felix Frankfurter, who worked with both men, has perhaps summed it up best when he recalled that

A divergence emerged between the rigorous, economically oriented outlook of Justice Brandeis and the entire consequence of the disciplined, even if inspired, mind that he was, and the kind of passionate, romantic quasi-messianic temperament of Weizmann so far as the realization of Herzl's dream of a Jewish Palestine. That doesn't mean that Weizmann wasn't shrewd, that he wasn't hard-headed, that he wasn't even in some respects cunning and crafty, and it doesn't mean that he wasn't a disciplined scientist, as he was, but when it came to the promotion of Zionist interests he wasn't preeminently a scientist. He was preeminently a man filled with a great dream which because of its adventuresomeness, daring to his mind and anyone's mind, required something more and beyond the careful calculation of an enterprise influenced by economic considerations, or the kind of hard-headed regard for details that was so characteristic of Mr. Justice Brandeis. That doesn't mean that Brandeis wasn't a dreamer too, but the whole bent of, not his temperament, but certainly what experience had done to his temperament, made him not oratorical, not passion stirring, not sky-scaling in his speech and even in his thinking, but made him so much more—what shall I say, well, disciplined is the word, than Weizmann. Different pressures had molded the two men. Brandeis's pressures were intellectual and the pressures of the imagination. They weren't the pressures of felt anti-Semitism, the pressures of the whole background of the Russian Pale, the pressures of actually being in communion with masses of Jews in Europe under the awful weight of squalid conditions, triumphing over them by a spiritual serenity.[41]

The primary aim of the Provisional Committee had been to facilitate relief to Jews afflicted by the war, and as long as the United States remained neutral, the Committee restricted itself to this goal. With American entry into the conflict in

April, 1917, however, the opportunities for more ambitious work became apparent. The Provisional Committee had been able to unite nearly all the different Zionist factions in a common goal, and under Brandeis's leadership, they now began to exert a greater influence in world Zionist affairs. Weizmann called on the now Mr. Justice Brandeis repeatedly to get the American government to respond to Zionist demands upon the British government. Brandeis followed the drafting of the Balfour Declaration closely and advised Wilson on certain changes necessary in the document, as well as urging him to approve the principle of a Jewish homeland in Palestine.[42] With the dream of restoration now assuming some substance, Brandeis, as usual, began to think in terms of just how to make that dream a reality.

Shortly after the publication of Balfour's letter to Lord Rothschild stating His Majesty's Government's approval of establishing a Jewish homeland in Palestine, Weizmann set up a Zionist Commission to go to Palestine to see how best to implement Jewish settlement there. Although Brandeis felt it impolitic to have American representation on the Commission, he wrote Weizmann that all care should be taken to preserve the land for the people:

> The utmost vigilance should be exercised to prevent the acquisition by private persons of land, water rights, or other national resources or any concessions for public utilities. These must all be secured for the whole Jewish people. In other ways, as well as this, the possibility of capitalistic exploitation must be guarded against. A high development of the Anglo-Palestine Company will doubtless prove one of the most effective means of protection. And the encouragement of all kinds of co-operative enterprises will be indispensable. Our pursuit must be primarily of agriculture in all its branches. The industries and commerce must be incidental merely—and such as may be required to insure independence and natural development.[43]

This neo-Jeffersonian faith was amplified by a five-point program adopted by the American Zionists at their convention in June, 1918. Drawn by Brandeis and known as the Pittsburgh

Program, it listed five points essential for the development of a
Jewish commonwealth:

> *First:* We declare for political and civil equality irrespec-
> tive of race, sex, or faith of all the inhabitants of the land.
> *Second:* To insure in the Jewish National Home in Pales-
> tine equality of opportunity we favor a policy which, with due
> regard to existing rights, shall tend to establish the ownership
> and control by the whole people of the land, of all natural re-
> sources and of all public utilities.
> *Third:* All the land, owned or controlled by the whole
> people, should be leased on such conditions as will insure the
> fullest opportunity for development and continuity of posses-
> sion.
> *Fourth:* The co-operative principle should be applied so
> far as feasible in the organization of all agricultural, in-
> dustrial, commercial, and financial undertakings.
> *Fifth:* The system of free public instruction which is to be
> established should embrace all grades and departments of edu-
> cation.[44]

Here indeed is the summation of progressive faith in the possibility of establishing a land of social justice and human
cooperation. Zionism, he had once written, should "represent
in Jewish life what Progressivism does in general American
life." [45]

This statement, however, reflected too much the progressivism that Brandeis sought to implant in Zionism. Despite its
idealism, and despite the fact that all of its provisions were ultimately adopted, it struck the Europeans as too secular a document. Where in it could one find anything Jewish? Despite the
fact that the Americans used the Pittsburgh program as the
basis for their versions of the proposed British mandate, the
European Zionists refused to accept it.

In 1919, Brandeis sailed for Europe and Palestine, to meet
with Weizmann and the other European leaders, as well as to
see Palestine for himself. In two weeks there, he traveled up
and down the land, examining everything, visiting nearly two
dozen of the Jewish colonies, and listening, listening to all who
could provide him with information. "The problems and the
difficulties are serious and numerous," he wrote to his wife,

"even more so than I had anticipated." [46] The practical obsta-
cles which he foresaw, however, would prove relatively simple
compared to the troublesome attitudes of the European Zionists.

In 1920, the Zionists met in World Conference for the first
time since before the war, and Brandeis again sailed for London to head the American delegation. Prior to the formal meetings, he met with Weizmann, Sokolow, and others to prepare a
plan for the development of Palestine. At Weizmann's suggestion, the Conference elected Brandeis as chairman, and at the
opening session, he set forth a plan to disband the old Zionist
apparatus, move all administrative functions to Palestine, and
to emphasize practical accomplishments rather than political
maneuverings. The old Actions Comité, the executive body of
the Zionists, would be replaced by a three-man executive committee, with full power and authority to get on with the work.
Brandeis ruled himself out of consideration for one of the
seats, since he would not resign from the Supreme Court. He
had long argued that a man could be both an American and a
Zionist; to leave the bench would give the lie to that belief.[47] If
it were desirable, he would serve as honorary president, a position from which he could advise the triumvirate without com-
promising his obligations to the Court.

Although Weizmann had evidently approved this plan at
their earlier meetings, the resulting uproar from his colleagues
led him to back off. Brandeis wanted the best possible executives to manage the development of Palestine, whether they
had been Zionists before or not; practical work required capable men. The Europeans resented this, since the plan took no
account of the Jewishness of Zionism. Weizmann later wrote:
"The World Zionist Organization, the Congresses, were not
just *ad hoc* instruments; they were the expression of the unity
of the Jewish people. The propositions of the Brandeis group,
dealing ostensibly with merely formal matters, with organizational instrumental rearrangements, actually reflected a denial
of Jewish nationalism; they made of Zionism simply a sociological plan ... instead of the folk renaissance that it was." [48]

Other Zionists charged that the Brandeis plan was another case of "Ugandism" and bitterly fought it.[49]

There was some truth to this charge that the Brandeisians failed to understand the nature of European Zionism, but if my argument is correct, it resulted not from a deliberate attempt to eliminate the Jewishness in Zionism, but from the peculiar circumstances of American Zionism itself. The progressive movement was idealistic, but it also had its feet firmly on the ground, and by the end of the war, could point to a long list of solid achievements in making American society a more just society.[50] It was not a case of opposing Jewishness, but one of emphasizing achievements in a long-term plan of development. The question of Jewishness was thus irrelevant. Jews would come, if they wished, to Palestine; the religious modes they might adopt would be up to them. But to get them there, and establish a commonwealth, required solid planning. If the Americans had had the gift of seeing the future, they might have realized that the idealistic impracticality and the emphasis on a rebirth of Jewish nationalism would be as important to the ultimate birth of Israel as their own demands for getting on with the work.

Brandeis left the London conference bitterly disappointed at what he considered Weizmann's betrayal. The Europeans had opted for what he believed to be a disastrous program, and now they had to accept the responsibility. The Americans, moreover, were no longer quite so willing to be financiers to the world movement, especially since Brandeis now mistrusted Weizmann's integrity in monetary management as well. At the end of the conference, over Brandeis's objections, a land-purchase fund had been created (*Keren Ha-yesod*) which would centralize all Zionist contributions in one agency.[51]

Brandeis had for years been unrelenting in his insistence that public as well as private organizations and businesses maintain the highest standards of fiscal responsibility. He had toppled the Morgan-backed New Haven by his disclosures of corruption and mismanagement, and had built up savings bank life insurance on the charges of illicit practices and waste in insurance companies. The *Keren Ha-yesod* mixed up all income, with no safeguards to distinguish between donations, operating funds, and investment. When Weizmann decided to challenge Brandeis on his own ground by establishing a *Keren Ha-yesod* in the United States, the stage was set for the final break between the two men.

The *Keren Ha-yesod* by itself could easily be interpreted as a minor issue, and, in truth, it did serve as a smokescreen to cover up more fundamental differences between American and European Zionism. But it also epitomized those differences. Weizmann wanted an agency that could appeal to all Jews, who would donate through a consciousness of their identity, and how it operated mattered very little to him. Brandeis, on the other hand, believed that the means related directly to the ends; broken promises and sloppy management hindered the establishment of the ultimate goal, a Jewish homeland in Palestine.

The dispute came to a head at the 1921 convention of the Zionist Organization of America in Cleveland. Weizmann personally led the opposition to the Brandeis regime, and capitalized on his own popularity, the latent dissent and jealousy in the American ranks, as well as the changed nature of the organization. In 1914, the Zionits had consisted primarily of Americanized Jews; by 1921, a large influx of eastern European immigrants had shifted the balance of membership to a stance more sympathetic with Weizmann's views. Louis Lipsky, one of Weizmann's lieutenants, described their following in Cleveland:

> These were the relatives of the Jews of Vilna, of Warsaw, of Bucharest, of Krakow and of Vienna. They were waiting for [Weizmann] to speak and they would rise and greet the historic opportunity he would describe. They were thirsting for his words. A leadership that could not speak to them in the language they understood, that persisted in going its own way without considering their feelings, prejudices and ideals, would not be able to lead them in the great period of building. These Jews declined to raise any barriers between Zionists in America and Zionists in Europe. They were not aware of any double loyalties. They had become Zionists through the

passion of their leaders in Russia, in Poland, and in Rou-
mania. They had not been separated from other Jews by time
and distance. They were not the lost tribes of Israel. They
were kinsmen who had wandered from home and who had
found freedom in a new land, but they remembered their origins.[52]

On a vote of confidence, the Brandeis group lost, 153 to 171.
Brandeis had anticipated this, and Judge Julian Mack read a
letter of resignation from the honorary president: "Strict adherence to those principles [adopted by the Executive Commit-
tee] is demanded by the high Zionist ideals. Steadfast pursuit
of those policies is essential to early and worthy development of
Palestine as the Jewish Homeland. We who believe in those
principles and policies cannot properly take part in any administration of Zionist affairs which repudiates them." Although
withdrawing from the leadership, they would not withdraw
from Zionism. "Our place will then be as humble soldiers in
the ranks where we may hope to hasten by our struggle the
coming of the day when the policies in which we believe will
be recognized as the only ones through which our great ends
may be achieved." [53] With Brandeis went the cream of the leadership, as Mack reported the resignation, name by name, of
thirty-seven members of the Executive Committee, including
himself, Israel Brodie, Bernard Flexner, Stephen S. Wise,
Jacob deHaas, Horace Kallen, Robert Szold, Harry Frieden-
wald, Abba Hillel Silver, Felix Frankfurter, Nathan Strauss,
and Julius Rosenwald. The Brandeis era of American Zionism
thus came to an end.

The feud between Brandeis and Weizmann never cleared,
and in the end, both men in large measure found justification
for their positions. Weizmann's pursuit of his incredible dream
inspired thousands of Jews to work for the establishment of Israel, and his insistence upon the necessity of a peculiarly Jewish homeland became tragically justified after the rise of Hitler
in the 1930s. Brandeis's idealism, though not as emotional or as
easily seen as Weizmann's, centered on his profound faith that
Palestine could be developed into a Jewish homeland.

The passage of time, moreover, saw the adoption of nearly all of Brandeis's proposals. Within a few months after the Cleveland fight, both Weizmann and Shmaryahu Levin told the Twelfth Zionist Congress that political maneuvering could now end, and that Zionists should get down to the solid, everyday, practical business of developing Palestine.[54] In the mid-thirties, a leading European historian of the movement declared that "on the whole it may be stated that most things demanded by Brandeis . . . gradually have been executed." [55]

If this is so, why then did there have to be such a bitter struggle, a struggle which robbed the movement of some of its most capable men for nearly a decade? In part, jealousy and misunderstanding undoubtedly existed between the two men. Weizmann had been a Jew of Jews, a Zionist all of his life, and had been active in the movement since the days of Herzl. He had slowly risen to become the head of the European Zionists, had been accepted as their spokesman by kings, sultans, and prime ministers, and now suddenly an assimilated, Americanized son of a freethinking deistic family rose to challenge his leadership and, for a brief moment, exercise greater power and authority than Weizmann had ever dreamed of attaining. Casting rhetoric aside at one point, Weizmann bluntly stated that the issue separating them was not the *Keren Ha-yesod,* but that "the fundamental question is, who shall control the work in Palestine. The American leaders wish to make themselves the rulers of the Zionist movement." [56]

The real differences, I would maintain, lay not in overt jealousy so much as in completely different conceptions of Jewish identity and the function of Zionism in Jewish life. For Weizmann, Zionism and Judaism were one and the same, and only "real Jews"—those of the masses—could understand what his dream meant: that it was more than a dream, it was a necessity for survival. To Brandeis, Zionism was an option, a means of maintaining a Jewish identity for those who wished to live in other parts of the world. The charge by one of Weizmann's followers that "Louis D. Brandeis would not be at home in the B'nai Brak colony in Palestine" [57] was perfectly true—and totally irrelevant.

Brandeis's Zionism was a function of his progressivism, a particular faith in the democratic process and in a just society. It also held that men should be free to live where they wished, free from irrational prejudices. The belief that all Jews should live in Palestine struck him as unsound and as unjust as any restrictive covenant or whispered bias. Zionism only made sense to him as a liberating movement, a process that would free the Jew and end the "Jewish problem." To Weizmann, Brandeis's solution might have seemed worse than the problem.

Chapter VI

THREADS FROM A PATTERN

In January, 1916, Woodrow Wilson stunned the country by nominating Louis Brandeis to the Supreme Court; only a handful of Administration figures and Senator Robert M. La-Follette had known ahead of time of the President's plans. The bitter fight that erupted between supporters and opponents of the nomination provided a good index of those who belonged in the broad stream of progressive reform and of those who did not. The nomination elicited a flood of newspaper and magazine articles, as well as thousands of letters to Congress and the White House, from proponents of wage and hour legislation, scientific management, conservation, unionism, municipal reform, child labor laws, and hosts of other projects, all of whom welcomed the opportunity to seat a known progressive on the Court.

For the most part, the anti-Brandeis attack reflected the fears that his past advocacy of controversial measures would threaten the Court's continued support of the status quo.[1] In addition, personal animosities on the part of those with whom he had fought, as well as some anti-Semitism, swelled the chorus of opposition. In few issues of this time can we find so stark a lineup of those who claimed the term "progressive" and those who clung tenaciously to things as they were.[2] Both sides recognized that Louis Dembitz Brandeis was a reformer of reformers, yet one whose innate conservatism, intellectual brilliance, and executive ability raised him far above the normal crowd of do-gooders.

Not all who supported Brandeis for the high court seat were without reservations; many would not deny him the honor, but they admitted that they would miss his energies and abilities in the good fight. Perhaps the best example of this sentiment lay in a letter from Amos Pinchot:

> Dear Louis:
>
> Although I have done what I could in the fight for your confirmation and earnestly desired it—still, now that you are actually a Supreme Court Justice, I don't know whether to be sorry or glad. So far, I think that I am sort of sorry.
>
> Yet I know that the same things that worry me must have worried you, and I know that you must have made plans to discount them. I know that you never would have accepted the judgeship, unless you were satisfied in your mind that you could escape the common fate of judges; that you could make the office very different from other judgeships. Nevertheless, I have a sinking spell when I think of your humanity subjective to the terrible test of remaining human under the black robe.
>
> Taking it all together, I don't think it is unfair to say that, for the last ten years, you have been the most vital and disturbing element in our public life. You have worked quietly, doing the unpopular things that reformers have talked and written about. You have made more trouble for injustice than any other man. The passing of your work, both light cavalry and heavy artillery, the knowledge that no longer, when a cause needs a great militant advocate, you will step forward as you have heretofore to fight the exploiters and debauchers of America's men, women and children, makes me feel pretty sad. As long as you were in private life, it seemed to me that, if any monstrous injustice should be attempted upon helpless people, they would not lack protection. You furnished to me personally, and to many people who are making the rather lonely fight against privilege, a kind of confidence that we will sorely miss. . . .[3]

This letter evidently touched Brandeis's inner thoughts, since he answered it at greater length than he did most of the congratulatory letters pouring in on him. "I can well appreciate what you say," he wrote, because it expresses to so large an extent what I myself have felt. It seemed to me upon full consideration that I was bound to accept the nomination when it was offered, although I realized fully what the relinquishments were which acceptance involved.

The doubts which I originally felt have been largely removed by the efforts of those who sought to defeat confirmation; and the responses which came from those less favored by fortune. The struggle certainly was worth while. It has defined the issues. It has been a great education to a large number of people; perhaps even to judges. And I trust it may prove possible for me to render service of real value on the Bench.[4]

Yet those, like Amos Pinchot, who feared that once on the Court Brandeis would withdraw from the various efforts to improve American society need not have worried; in the quarter century left to his remarkable life, Brandeis remained a constant source of inspiration and encouragement, and on several occasions actively joined the fight.

On the bench, Brandeis stood as a model of judicial propriety. He would never discuss cases pending before the Court with an outsider, nor would he comment on decisions after they had been reached. Despite an endless flow of letters from well-wishers and admirers concerning his decisions and/or dissents, he rarely responded, and when he did, it usually consisted of little more than a brief and formal acknowledgment.[5] He even refused to accept the many honorary degrees tendered to him, on the grounds that the proprieties of the office precluded such honors. In his private affairs, he continued investing his large estate in conservative utility bonds, after conferring with Chief Justice Edward White to be sure that this would not, under any circumstances, be construed as a possible conflict of interests.[6]

Formally, he resigned from many of his reform activities, with certain significant exceptions. There was, of course, Zionism, which held his interest and attention until his death. He also continued to support, both with advice and money, savings bank life insurance, which he considered his most important effort. His private secretary, Miss Alice H. Grady, became Deputy Commissioner in charge of the program in 1920, and over the next fifteen years consulted frequently with her ex-employer.[7] He also maintained his interest in building up the University of Louisville,[8] and the well-being of his beloved Harvard Law School never failed to elicit a response. Working through Felix Frankfurter, Brandeis kept well informed of the School's activities, and each year rewarded one of its brighter students with an appointment as clerk.

These, however, were all within the bounds of normally acceptable behavior for a Supreme Court justice; at no time did Brandeis ever indulge in the out-and-out political maneuvering that William Howard Taft so enjoyed during his tenure as Chief Justice.[9] Yet beneath the surface Brandeis was an off-the-court activist with few peers in this century. He served as an effective and influential advisor to both the Wilson and Roosevelt Administrations, and was in constant touch with officials from the President on down. But he husbanded his resources, acted discreetly, moved only when he believed he could be of assistance, and preferred to be sought out by the Administration rather than go to them.

Wilson, for one, could not afford to have Brandeis isolated on the Court. During the nomination fight, the President had written to Senator Charles A. Culberson:

> I have tested [Brandeis] by seeking his advice upon some of the most difficult and perplexing public questions about which it was necessary for me to form a judgment. I have dealt with him in matters where nice questions of honor and fair play, as well as large questions of justice and public benefit, were involved. In every matter in which I have made test of his judgment and point of view I have received from him counsel singularly enlightening, singularly clear-sighted and judicial, and, above all, full of moral stimulation.[10]

As America was drawn into the First World War, Wilson time and again found that he needed Brandeis's advice. No one, it seemed, could take his place as counsel to the President. Within a few weeks after Brandeis had taken his seat on the bench, Wilson asked him to go to Mexico as head of a border commission to settle disputes with Carranza. After consultation with the Chief Justice, Brandeis declined on the grounds that the appointment would be inconsistent with his duties on the Court.[11]

Several times during the next three years Wilson would be urged to appoint Brandeis as dictator of the railroads or head of the War Labor Board or chief of the peace delegation to Paris. "I need Brandeis everywhere," Wilson told Stephen Wise.[12] Another time, the President informed Robert Wooley that "when a seemingly impossible war emergency task looms, I am urged to draft Brandeis to tackle it. At least twice I have put it up to him. Very properly he replied that he would take it up with the Chief Justice. In each instance Chief Justice White held that a member of the Supreme Court should confine his endeavors to the work of the Court. I readily agreed. Whereupon Brandeis would offer to resign, which was characteristic of him. My reply was: 'Not on your life. On that Bench you are more important to the Country than you could possibly be elsewhere. It was too difficult to get you there to take a chance on losing you through a temporary arrangement.' " [13]

But if Wilson could not utilize Brandeis's many talents openly, he nonetheless secured his counsel privately. Both he and many of his subordinates in various agencies were prone to call on the Justice when a particularly difficult problem posed itself.[14] In the fall of 1917, Brandeis was instrumental in convincing the President to name William Gibbs McAdoo to head the nation's railroad system. Later that winter a problem of great urgency confronted the Administration. Woodrow Wilson and many of his advisors were both ideologically and politically unsuited to the task of running a modern war. Its basic premises of restricted government, small-unit economics, and competition rather than cooperation might have been suitable for a peacetime economy and society. War, however, demanded centralized governmental operations and control, large-scale production, and the elimination of waste, especially the wastes of competition. In 1913, Wilson had appointed men who had agreed with his ideology, regardless of their particular competence. Josephus Daniels knew nothing about a navy, William Jennings Bryan even less about international diplomacy, but both had strongly supported the tenets of Wilson's program. The outbreak of war caused not only a reexamination of policy, but demanded that expertise, not ideology, figure prominently in key decisions.[15]

Wilson slowly came to realize this, and his agonies were not made lighter by the realization that during the war, much of what he had fought for would have to be shelved, at least temporarily. Moreover, once done, it would not be easy to revivify those programs after the fighting had stopped. Theodore Roosevelt had already proclaimed that if the Sherman Act were bad for the country during wartime, then surely it must be equally as bad at other times.[16] As the industrial war machine bogged down, the Administration came under increasing pressure to appoint wartime "czars" to exercise central authority over the economy. Wilson, aware of the need for more production, yet still holding to his beliefs in a competitive economy and fearful of central authority, turned, as he often did, to Brandeis.

This time the medium of exchange was Colonel Edward M. House, the President's confidant, who asked Brandeis what should be done. The Justice replied in a lengthy letter confirming the increasing need for a greater centralized power. "The powers of the munitions administration shall be vested in a single head with full powers of delegation; and the delegated power shall likewise be vested in single officials with full power of action within the sphere delimited. . . . There shall be no committees within the munitions administration except such advisory committees as the official shall himself appoint for his aid. The sphere of action of the several officials shall be limited to a size consistent with efficient action by him. . . ." He went on to urge that the War Department should be restricted to running the war, rather than running industry and having to deal with the many problems of procurement. Each branch should do what it had to, and nothing beyond that.[17]

Although at first reading one could interpret this advice as going contrary to all that Brandeis had previously stood for, a careful rereading makes it quite clear that he had again held true to his first principles. He was not so closed-minded to pretend, the way some of Wilson's advisors did, that the country could go on undisturbed during the war. New crises demanded new approaches, but basic principles could be sustained. Where others saw the problems in terms of centralizing power and increasing the activities of government, Brandeis urged clear lines of responsibility. Men were trying to do too much; just as he had inveighed against businessmen taking on too many tasks, so he now declared that administrators also had to restrict themselves to what they could accomplish. The recommendations, as he noted, "rest largely upon the obvious limitation of the power of any one man to deal effectively with many extensive and difficult problems. It is only by freeing Secretary [of War Newton D.] Baker from many of the burdens now improperly resting upon him that the country can get the full benefit of his great ability and fine qualities." [18]

Where others thought the confusion resulted from insufficient power, Brandeis viewed it in the additional context of responsibility. Here the champion of scientific management declared that the government already had the necessary powers, but had failed to utilize them effectively. The answer lay not in granting more power—the Presidency was overburdened with power. What had to be done was to delineate specifically who would do what, give that person the necessary latitude and authority, and then hold him strictly accountable for performance in that area; in other words, to rationalize administration. Man, especially in wartime, could be overwhelmed by the magnitude of his work.

The higher call of service to the country in wartime may have justified Brandeis's extrajudicial role of counsel to the President of the United States. But what shall we say about serving as partisan advocate to the head of the Democratic party? For Mr. Justice Brandeis frequently advised courses necessary for the good of the party as well as of the country; in fact, at times he seemed to believe that the future well-being of the Democratic party and of the United States were one and inseparable.

Originally a Republican, Brandeis had always voted independently, and his various pressure-group reform organizations in Massachusetts had supported friendly legislators and councilmen on a nonpartisan basis. He had had very little quarrel with the policies of Theodore Roosevelt, especially since the Democratic party at the time had been led by William Jennings Bryan, with some of whose policies he strongly disagreed. But after 1909, Brandeis had grown increasingly disillusioned by the Grand Old Party, especially by the political blunderings of the Taft Administration during the Pinchot-Ballinger affair. The Taft wing of the party, he believed, had come under the total domination of the Wall Street moneylenders and spokesmen of big business, and at one point he had lamented: "If only there were a Democratic Party, what havoc could be wrought." [19] Although he had originally supported Wisconsin's Robert M. LaFollette, Brandeis had found his leader in Woodrow Wilson, and had been an active Democrat since the summer of 1912.

From March, 1913, on, Brandeis had advised the President not only on economic policy, but also on patronage, frequently recommending appointments in the Massachusetts area and in federal agencies. Once he was on the Court, this type of activity ceased, although Brandeis occasionally suggested men for jobs in various wartime agencies during the war. In the summer of 1916, the Justice submitted a draft plank on preparedness to Wilson for the Democratic platform.[20] In his letter to Colonel House suggesting administrative reorganization, Brandeis made it quite clear that party fortunes rested upon successful prosecution of the war. "I consider the situation very serious," he noted, "imperilling success abroad and also the ascendancy of the Democratic Party upon which we must rely for the attainment of our ideals at home." [21]

Wilson left the White House in March, 1921, seemingly broken politically, physically, and mentally. Carefully nursed by his wife and a small coterie of relatives and friends, the ex-

President soon threw off the outward symptoms of depression, although remaining quite weak. Within a few months, Wilson's idealism began asserting itself, and for the next two years until his death, he again turned to that moral exhortation that, as the son of a Presbyterian minister, he had always believed to be the most effective of all political weapons. Together with a handful of other Wilson confidants, Mr. Justice Brandeis worked to draft a radically progressive platform that they hoped would unite the Democratic party and carry it to victory in 1924. Few statements sum up New Freedom progressivism so clearly and eloquently as does the "Document," as the results of their joint efforts came to be known.

The idea of the "Document" evidently germinated in conversations between Wilson and Brandeis in early June, 1921; the ex-President then asked Brandeis to contact Bainbridge Colby and Thomas L. Chadbourne "to confer on some matters affecting labor and industry." [22] Wilson, restless after so many years of activity, seemed unable to contain his thoughts, and began writing bits and snatches on a variety of topics, which he then sent to Brandeis for comment. The very first statement, on foreign affairs, bitterly attacked "the most partisan, prejudiced and unpatriotic coterie that has ever misled the Senate of the United States," and called for immediate resumption of America's role in world leadership.[23]

By early winter statements had been rough-drafted on a number of topics, including foreign policy, development of a merchant marine, agriculture, labor, and the control of big business. Wilson did most of the original writing, with Brandeis and Colby constantly criticizing and amending the material. In January, 1922, several more veterans of the Wilson Administration, including David F. Houston and Bernard Baruch, were called in to discuss the "Document," which reached its final form in April.

As much as any written statement can, the "Document" sums up, as it were, what Brandeis and Wilson and other supporters of the New Freedom had been striving for since 1912: a mature, total commitment to the kind of society they wanted, and the place in the world they wanted the United States to occupy. It was, above all, an internationalist statement, for its framers warned that we could never again retreat into isolation from the other nations of the world. Rather, we had the responsibility to use our wealth and industrial strength to help build a strong and free world, since only in that kind of world could peace be maintained. "We demand," they said, "the immediate resumption of our international obligations and leadership."

While they still paid tribute to the concept of competition, the writers had evidently learned the lessons of the war. Although domination by capital was still condemned, there was more talk of coordination and cooperation, especially between capital and labor. In a section obviously written by Brandeis, the "Document" called for laws allowing retail fair-price agreements, a device the author believed would maintain a competitive economy. There was also a slight tinge of people's socialism in the "Document," with a clear statement that all resources ultimately belonged to the people, and must, therefore, be administered for their benefit.

In the "Document" can be found reliance upon the initiative of the people, a belief that equal opportunity within the economic and social systems must be maintained, the necessity for curbing greed, and now a new note, a missionary zeal for spreading this remarkable system throughout the world. But there is also a hard, biting, indeed bitter edge, a combativeness that would have sounded strange in 1912, a partisanship almost as strong as that which they attacked.[24]

The "Document" never received a wide circulation. Wilson had several times tried to devise some means by which the ideas could be aired or presented to the Democratic party as its platform. For a while, he had hoped to have every Democrat up for election in 1922 pledge themselves to this testament; their victory, he had believed, would thus stand as a vindication of his own ideas and policies.[25] No one, however, seemed to know exactly what to do with the "Document" once it had been written, and Wilson died in 1923 before any action could be taken.

It is, perhaps, just as well that the "Document," had it been

made public, did not become a basis for what would have undoubtedly been a divisive battle within the party. After two
decades of reform at home and battle abroad, the American
people had had their share of idealism and sacrifice. The election of Warren Harding in 1920 was only in part a rebuff of
Wilson; the electorate resoundingly approved the "normalcy"
that Harding promised to them.[26] In 1924, and again in 1928,
this demand to be let alone would be reiterated, and the Democrats would grope among themselves for some sort of party
identification.

Brandeis's role in preparing the "Document" would have
undoubtedly drawn a great deal of fire; extrajudicial activities
so blatantly political would have been repugnant to most
Americans. But the real questions that have to be faced deal
with the bounds of judicial propriety, and whether or not
Louis Brandeis exceeded them.

Persons appointed to judicial office are named only in part
for their judicial capabilities and potential. Men like Oliver
Wendell Holmes, Jr., and Benjamin Cardozo had been recognized as brilliant jurists before their appointment to the Supreme Court, but Brandeis, Felix Frankfurter, William Howard Taft, George Sutherland, and Harlan Fiske Stone all
received their seats partially as a reward for service faithfully
rendered. In addition, they all had the "potential" for becoming jurists. The fact that many "political" appointees turn out
to be excellent, in fact distinguished, members of a court
should surprise no one; after all, the sagacity and balance and
temperament which we prize in judges we also seek in those to
whom we turn for advice.

The Supreme Court cannot and should not be isolated
from the mainstream of public affairs, especially when its decisions can decisively alter or reshape that mainstream. If the
Court, for example, is to lay down school desegregation guidelines, should the judges be totally unaware of the very real
problems confronting schoolboards on this issue? Much of the
current attack on the courts revolves around their total disregard for practical difficulties involved in desegregating schools
or revising criminal procedures. Brandeis himself, in his ad-

dress on "The Living Law," had charged that a good deal of what was wrong with the courts lay in the isolation from and ignorance of the real world which characterized so many judges.[27]

If the high court supposedly provides security for the judges from the political repercussions of their decisions, then it must also provide them a greater sense of detachment and of objectivity. Perhaps no better guidance can come than from one who has no personal stake in the outcome, whose ambitions have been sated, whose vulnerability has been shielded. We must strip away this self-righteous mask and admit that the men we want to see in the highest court, indeed in all high governmental positions, are there because of a number of qualifications. Wilson had asserted that Brandeis's counsel had been very wise, and senators had accepted that as one legitimate reason for his approval. Once on the Court, should the country be limited to having that counsel expressed solely in majority decisions or minority dissents?

The question becomes stickier once we come to the question of partisan political activity as opposed to services concerning national policy. The Supreme Court was designed to shield men from paying political consequences for their courage and integrity in upholding the Constitution as they saw it. Their tenure does not shield them from their own personal avarice or mistakes, and it should not protect them if they desire to engage in partisan manipulation. The country would have been rightly upset if it had discovered a Supreme Court justice working to draft a party platform in order to get the Democrats back into power. We expect, and rightly so, an Olympian detachment when it comes to partisan politics, and on this count Brandeis violated his own concepts of judicial propriety.[28]

Throughout the 1920s, Brandeis was indeed a voice crying in the wilderness, both on and off the bench. Almost alone save for Holmes, and later for Harlan Fiske Stone, he fired off dissents that served as powerful reminders that the law must march in hand with progress. Privately, he continued to urge economic and social reforms, despite the "fact" that permanent prosperity had apparently arrived with the Republicans. He especially prodded Paul Kellogg and the *Survey* Associates to continue investigating the problems of irregular employment. When the crash came, people suddenly rediscovered Brandeis the reformer. An inexpensive edition of *Other People's Money* received wide circulation, while numerous magazine articles cited his words. And in 1933, the new occupant of the White House, together with many of his advisors, sought advice from Brandeis, whom Franklin Roosevelt called "Isaiah."

Brandeis was not totally happy with the New Deal at first. The President's preoccupation with recovery forced those who were primarily interested in economic reform to the side. Roosevelt seemed unwilling to tie the two together and demanded that the economy perk up before major innovative reforms be attempted. Like many who had served in the World War, Roosevelt considered the wartime experience a useful model for dealing with the Depression.[29] The so-called First New Deal, as a result, emphasized cooperation, efficiency, and bigness—all tempered by administrators who still believed in the New Nationalism.

By mid-1934, however, as Roosevelt began to realize that reform and recovery had to proceed together, the Administration began to wrestle with many of the problems that Brandeis had attacked three decades earlier. The failure of the National Recovery Administration revived antitrust sentiment, and the Public Utilities Holding Company Act broke up some of the monopolistic trends in public power. Various securities laws imposed long-needed regulation on Wall Street and greatly reduced the ability of money manipulators to play with other people's money.

Brandeis's influence during the New Deal operated both directly and indirectly. Roosevelt consulted him on several occasions, and Brandeis played a key role in shaping the Wagner-Lewis and Social Security acts, with their emphases on shared responsibility between the states and the Federal government.[30] More pervasive was his indirect influence upon numerous middle- and lower-rank officials, especially the young-

sters Felix Frankfurter kept sending down from the Harvard
Law School. Evenings and Sundays they would come to his
apartment for either dinner or tea and discuss their problems
with him, filling him in on the latest political maneuverings
and administrative or ideological difficulties. According to one
who vividly remembers the scene, the Justice never suggested
what solutions should be, but elicited so much information and
asked such coherent questions that when the young New
Dealer rose to leave, he or she would suddenly realize that they
had reached the answer.[31] Within the Administration, a loyal
coterie of neo-Brandeisians soon rose to occupy positions of vast
influence and power.[32] And, of course, from the bench he continued to use the law as a great educational instrument.

When the most celebrated advocate of his time took the
black silk robe of the nation's highest judicial body, many people wondered whether he could make so drastic a transition,
whether his combative nature, his free spirit and individualism, would ever settle into the restrictive harness of Court procedure. As one of his clerks later wrote: "As practitioner, a
feared opponent and valiant champion, master of technique
and not mastered by it, daring, adroit, sometimes ruthless in attack, yet holding to principle: what in the practice of such a
man must the biographer find to explain why the judge could
cast off the partisan robe so completely?"[33] What indeed lay
inside the man that not only did he become a great member of
that Court, but that even those colleagues with whom he disagreed could testify to the fact that he served the Court exceedingly well?

Felix Frankfurter once wrote that "to quote from Mr. Justice Brandeis' opinions is not to pick plums from a pudding
but to pull threads from a pattern."[34] It is not my intention
here to explore in detail Brandeis's judicial career; that has
been done, and done well, in numerous other places. Rather, I
would like to pick out a few "threads from a pattern" to show
that once on the bench, Brandeis still maintained the older
principles and priorities, and that when two or more of his ten-

ets may have conflicted, he retained a clear sense of what was most important.

Brandeis quickly established himself as the ablest legal craftsman the Court has known in this century. His first dissent, involving the scope of a federal law, established the mode. Not only would he state what he considered the necessary legal points, but he would buttress them with an analysis of relevant facts and the reasoning behind the statute.[35] Charles Evans Hughes later described Brandeis as the "master of both microscope and telescope," [36] recognizing that Brandeis not only wanted the overall perspective, but demanded the close-up world of facts and analysis as well. While we may turn more often to Holmes for this pithy phrase or that Jovian pronouncement, we refer to Brandeis for the law, and for the hard facts and difficult reasoning behind the law.

As judge, Brandeis demanded of himself the same type of craftsmanship he had practiced as a lawyer. Craftsmanship meant more than just writing an able opinion or dissent, one in which ambiguity would be minimal. It meant searching out all of the relevant materials of any sort, be they legal, economic, or sociological, and then seeing how the law meshed with the facts.[37] Just as he had shown lawyers how to use this sort of data in the *Muller* brief, now he would try to impress upon his colleagues the necessity of understanding and evaluating the real world while handing down legal dicta from their sanctuary.

Because so much of the Court's business at the time involved economic questions, Brandeis appeared particularly well-qualified to inject some life into the law. "No man of his generation," wrote Harold Laski, "so fully understood the inner workings of the economic system." [38] His old love of facts and then more facts, a quality that had made him a brilliant lawyer, contributed to his greatness as a judge. One of the best exampes of Brandeis utilizing his economic understanding and background can be found in his concurring opinion in *Southwestern Bell Telephone Company v. Public Service Commis-*

sion of Missouri, a statement characterized by one economist as the ablest critique made on the economics of utility valuation.[39]

When states had first passed legislation regulating public utilities, the courts, practicing judicial restraint, had declined to interfere with the administrative agencies.[40] By 1898, however, not only had the Court decided that it would interfere, but in *Smyth v. Ames* arrogated unto judicial review the whole question of what constituted "fair" and "reasonable" rates.[41] The Court declared that under the aegis of the Fourteenth Amendment, public utility companies would be deprived of property without due process unless they received a fair return on their property. While few had quarreled with that premise, the Court had gone on to establish a formula based on current valuation of the property as the basis for establishing a fair rate. The problem here lay in the fact that current valuation was exceedingly difficult to determine. Moreover, if a company felt the regulatory agency had not been sufficiently generous, it could appeal the decision to the courts. A determined company could emasculate the state or local agency by appealing decisions to the courts, claiming deprivation of property without due process. Not only were judges frequently more sympathetic to the corporate viewpoint than to regulatory commissions, but also the expertise to evaluate the data was more marked by its absence than by its presence in the courts.

In 1922, the Supreme Court reversed the Missouri Supreme Court, which had upheld a Public Service Commission order reducing telephone rates. Mr. Justice McReynolds, in delivering the opinion, charged that the Commission's directed rates did not provide a fair return upon invested capital, and that it had been especially negligent in its valuation of the company's property as a basis for return, according to the formula in *Smyth v. Ames.* Brandeis, while concurring in the decision, announced, "I differ fundamentally from my brethren concerning the rule to be applied in determining whether a prescribed rate is confiscatory." He then went on to attack the whole basis of present value as a criteria for return.

By carefully tracing economic trends, Brandeis demonstrated how any attempt to determine current value could only end in chaos. Prices fluctuated from year to year, even from week to week. Since the worth of a utility depended to large measure on its earnings, and its earnings upon its rates, and its rates upon its value, the whole enterprise became one vicious circle. Relentlessly elaborating upon every defect in the system, Brandeis tried to show that the old rule, while it may have had some legal justification, just did not make any sense economically.

Characteristically, Brandeis did not stop with just an attack on a faulty system, but went on to propose a constructive alternative in its place. Drawing upon his experience with the Public Franchise League and the Interstate Commerce Commission, he suggested the adoption of "the prudent investment principle," which would assure a return commensurate with that of private capital prudently invested. While this method had its own complexities, it also had the benefit of a more easily ascertainable rate, and one which broke down the cycle of value–return–rate–value. Moreover, once methods and standards had been arrived at, the courts could withdraw from involvement in the regulatory procedure, and leave the administrative agencies as the prime instruments of control.

Brandeis's support of the "prudent investment principle" [42] had evolved logically from his earlier work in Massachusetts and with the I.C.C. He had always believed that private capital invested in public utilities deserved a fair return, but, because of the special status of a business affected with the public interest, great care had to be taken that the return remained fair and not exorbitant. He had crusaded for years to get state agencies and the I.C.C. to adopt modern and uniform principles of accounting, and to agree on fair and reasonable formulas which would be easily understandable and ascertainable, in justice to both investors and to the public.

Few of his colleagues accepted the "prudent investment principle" as a sound basis for rate-making, or even his legal arguments as to where the prime responsibility for regulation lay, the agencies or the courts. Pierce Butler, a former railroad attorney, probably understood some of Brandeis's arguments, but he viewed the Court as a bastion of protection for railroads and other businesses against the semisocialistic commissions. The rest of the Court displayed great ignorance about the economics of the matter. Even Holmes, who frequently joined Brandeis, did so more out of his faith in judicial restraint than in an understanding of the data.[43]

One of Brandeis's primary concerns before ascending the bench had been the "curse of bigness," and his judicial writings indicate that he maintained this passion after 1916. His faith in the benefits of smallness can be seen in various decisions concerning the regulation of business: in cases involving distinctions between large and small companies, he nearly always supported the right of the legislatures to make that differentiation.

In 1928, the Quaker City Cab Company challenged a Pennsylvania statute that imposed a tax on corporations engaged in intrastate transportation. Since many taxis belonged either to individuals or to partnerships, they escaped the tax, and the company claimed that this violated the Fourteenth Amendment's guarantee of equal protection. The Court, by a 6-to-3 vote, struck down the law, accepting the argument that an arbitrary distinction reflected no real differentiation between types, and thus failed to provide equal protection.[44]

In his dissent, Brandeis first addressed himself to the question of whether the distinction could be held reasonable, and decided in the affirmative. He then listed those attributes which made classification unacceptable, and found none of them present in the case. While normally satisfied that a legislature could use its own judgment within constitutionally prescribed bounds, Brandeis in this case went into some of the reasons behind the law, and in so doing, spoke as much for himself as he did for the Pennsylvania legislature:

> In Pennsylvania the practice of imposing heavier burdens upon corporations dates from a time when there, as elsewhere in America, the fear of growing corporate power was common. The present heavier imposition may be a survival of an early effort to discourage the resort to that form of organization. The apprehension is now less common. But there are still in-

telligent, informed, just-minded and civilized persons who believe that the rapidly growing aggregation of capital through
corporations constitutes an insidious menace to the liberty of
the citizen; that it tends to increase the subjection of labor to
capital; that, because of the guidance and control necessarily
exercised by great corporations upon those engaged in business, individual initiative is being impaired and creative
power will be lessened; that the absorption of capital by corporations, and their perpetual life, may bring evils similar to
those which attended mortmain; that the evils incident to the
accelerating absorption of business by corporations outweigh
the benefits thereby secured; and that the process of absorption should be retarded.[45]

Similarly, we find Brandeis's economic inclinations shining
through in *Liggett v. Lee,* in which a majority of the Court
held a Florida tax on chain stores invalid, also on the grounds
that it violated the equal protection clause.[46] The statute involved laid a heavier tax per store on owners operating in more
than one county than on those whose operations were restricted to one county. The obvious purpose of the law had
been to protect local operators against national chains. Mr. Justice Roberts, speaking for the Court, declared, "We are unable
to discover any reasonable basis for this classification."

To Brandeis, of course, the statute seemed more than reasonable, and almost reflexively he sprang to its defense. In a
forty-page dissent, he not only defended the Florida tax on constitutional grounds, but on its social merits as well. Business,
he declared, must yield to the public interest. "Businesses may
become as harmful to the community by excessive size, as by
monopoly or the commonly recognized restraints of trade. If
the State should conclude that bigness in retail merchandising
as manifested in corporate chain stores menaces the public welfare, it might prohibit the excessive size or extent of that business as it prohibits excessive size or weight in motor trucks or
excessive heights in the buildings of a city." [47]

He then went on to analyze the broader social implications of the tax, and, according to one scholar, "it would be
hard to find in judicial literature an utterance to compare with
its powerful exposition of the ramifying effects of the corporate

system." [48] Lest he be accused of injecting his own biases, Brandeis prefaced his accusations by ascribing them to "able, discerning scholars," and then recounted the evils that resulted from economic concentration—separation of ownership from control, dulling of individual initiative, inequality of opportunity, and so on. "The true prosperity of our past," he proclaimed in echoes of 1912, "came not from big business, but through the courage, the energy, and the resourcefulness of small men; that only by releasing from corporate control the faculties of the unknown many, only by reopening to them the opportunities for leadership, can confidence in our future be restored and the existing misery be overcome." [49]

If we sought out only those cases where Brandeis's opinions or dissents mirrored his earlier social, political, or economic views, we might easily conclude that he was as guilty as his more conservative brethren in erecting his personal beliefs into judicial fiat. Certainly there is evidence for this type of charge, and not just in the cases. Had not Holmes declared in 1881 that "the prejudices which judges share with their fellowmen" had more to do with shaping the law than did legal logic? [50] If guilty, then Brandeis must come in for his share of criticism, just as we have taken Taft, McReynolds, Butler, Sutherland, and the other conservatives to task for their insistence on injecting their own prejudices into the workings of the Court; because Brandeis may have stood on the liberal side will not leave him blameless.

Certainly no intelligent person will claim that Brandeis was a "passionless thinking machine," [51] who never allowed his own beliefs to creep into his writings. But, unlike some of his colleagues, Brandeis never allowed his priorities to become confused. He disliked bigness and championed competition, yet he also believed that in some circumstances competition had to be restricted. In 1921, therefore, he wrote one of his more powerful dissents in defense of an "open competition plan" designed to limit pure competition.[52] A group of hardwood manufacturers had agreed to exchange information about prices, production, and sales. Following the tenets of the "New Competition," this plan shifted emphasis from price competition to service and quality. Six members of the Court held the arrangement to be in restraint of trade, and Mr. Justice Clarke described it as "an expansion of the gentlemen's agreement of former days, skillfully devised to evade the law." [53]

Brandeis strongly disagreed, and declared that the "Sherman Law does not prohibit every lessening of competition; and it certainly does not command that competition be pursued blindly.... It is lawful to regulate competition in some degree." The apostle of competition, although seemingly eschewing it here, demonstrated both his flexibility as well his understanding of the intricacies of the market place. In his dissent, he made it quite clear that unless some sort of regulation were imposed, the ultimate result would probably be the lessening of competition through combination:

> The refusal to permit a multitude of small rivals to cooperate, as they have done here, in order to protect themselves and the public from the chaos and havoc wrought in their trade by ignorance, may result in suppressing competition in the hardwood industry.... May not these hardwood lumber concerns, frustrated in their efforts to rationalize competition, be led to enter the inviting field of consolidation? And if they do, may not another huge trust with highly centralized control over vast resources ... become so powerful as to dominate competitors, wholesalers, retailers, consumers, employees and, in large measure, the community? [54]

Brandeis displayed on a number of occasions this flexibility of mind that allowed him to see more than just the surface issue on hand. Had he functioned at the level of some of his colleagues, he might have struck out blindly at any attempt to lessen competition, as they struck out at all forms of social legislation. Rather, he realistically noted that sometimes, in order to save competition, it must be restricted; his advice to Wilson, after all, had been that in order to avoid monopoly, competition had to be regulated.

Even more important than his attentiveness to competition was his adherence to the principles of a federal system, and his belief that within that system, the Supreme Court had an important, but well-defined, role to play. No member of the

Supreme Court, wrote Frankfurter, "invoke [d] more rigor-
ously the traditional limits of its jurisdiction." [55] The Court
should never attempt to answer anything other than the immediate and narrowly defined question before it. "It is usually
more important," Brandeis wrote, "that a rule of law be settled,
than that it be settled right. Even where the error in declaring
the rule is a matter of serious concern, it is ordinarily better to
seek correction by legislation. Often this is true although the
question is a constitutional one." [56] His insistence on maintaining a proper balance of powers and obligations could sometimes
lead him into seemingly strange postures. As Paul Freund
noted, "Brandeis was prepared to reject the claims, almost lit-
erally, of a workman, a widow and an orphan in pursuance of
what seemed to him a more harmonious federalism." [57]

As with most men of strong beliefs and firm principles, occasions arose where two or more tenets of his faith might be in
conflict. One such case illustrates how Brandeis resolved this
conflict, and how well set were his priorities. The case involved
an Oklahoma statute requiring anyone entering the ice business to obtain a certificate of public convenience and necessity.
When a man named Liebman sought to open an ice company
without a certificate, the duly licensed New State Ice Company
sued to restrain him. Mr. Justice Sutherland, speaking for the
Court, found the Oklahoma law unconstitutional. In his decision, he attacked the statute on the grounds that it "does not
protect against monopoly, but tends to foster it. The aim is not
to encourage competition, but to prevent it; not to regulate the
business, but to preclude persons from engaging in it." [58] An
attack of this nature would have seemed more appropriate coming from Brandeis, yet in this case he wrote one of his ablest
dissents.

As to Sutherland's charge of fostering monopoly, Brandeis
merely stated that the power to terminate operation by revok-
ing the certificate actually served as a deterrent to the more oppressive practices normally associated with monopoly. Those
who might wonder if he had abandoned his faith in competition for the policy of regulated monopoly failed to perceive
that a more important issue at stake was the proper balance of

powers and limitations within the federal system. Brandeis may or may not have agreed with the reasoning behind the Oklahoma statute: that in a depression it was necessary to limit certain types of business for the public interest. He did recognize, however, that the state was attempting to deal with the depression in a new and experimental manner, and that under the police power, it had that right. "It is one of the happy incidents of the federal system that a single courageous State may, if its citizens choose, serve as a laboratory, and try novel social and economic experiments without risk to the rest of the country." [59]

In a federal system, power must be dispersed to the states, a concept certainly not strange for the opponent of concentration of power of any sort. The Court, however, also shared power in that system, and Brandeis demanded that it restrict itself to very limited functions. The Court may or may not have agreed with the aims of the Oklahoma statute, but that did not matter, and he appealed to his brethren to allow the system to be innovative and adaptive:

> This Court has the power to prevent an experiment. We may strike down the statute which embodies it on the ground that, in our opinion, the measure is arbitrary, capricious or unreasonable. We have the power to do this, because the due process clause has been held by the Court applicable to matters of substantive law as well as to matters of procedure. But in the exercise of this high power, we must be ever on our guard, lest we erect our prejudices into legal principles. If we would guide by the light of reason, we must let our minds be bold.[60]

At the apex of Brandeis's priorities stood the freedom of the individual. His lifelong battle against bigness and concentration did not imply attacking only economic power, but also the centralization of power in big government. Just as his federalism flowed naturally from his fear of the "curse of bigness," so his intense concern for civil liberties developed from both his federalism and his antipathy to concentrated power.

Although Holmes had led the way, especially in the area of free speech, various scholars have maintained that Brandeis understood the problems of civil liberties more fully, and pursued their defense more seriously, than did Holmes.[61] The reason, it would seem, was that Brandeis feared the encroachment of the state much more than Holmes did. "In every extension of governmental functions," warned Brandeis, "lurks a new danger to civil liberty." [62]

Together with Holmes, Brandeis fought against encroachments by the government, and the two of them stood almost alone throughout the 1920s. Beginning with the Abrams case,[63] the two men fought a long and seemingly losing battle to protect the right of people to criticize the government or to express different, and in some cases radical, views of society. Where Holmes was a civil libertarian because of his overwhelming devotion to the abstract realm of free ideas, Brandeis acted in accordance with his belief in the nature of a free society. "Men may differ widely as to what loyalty to our country demands," he wrote, "and an intolerant majority, swayed by passion or by fear, may be prone in the future, as it has often been in the past, to stamp as disloyal opinions with which it disagrees." [64] If the society were to survive, it had to allow those unhappy with the status quo the right to try to change it peacefully. Should the government insist that such efforts constituted unlawful incitement merely because a number of people did not share the minority views, and by silencing them forced the dissidents underground, then violent change might very well be the result.[65]

It may be that Brandeis's most eloquent statement in defense of individual rights came not in dissent, but in his concurring opinion in *Whitney v. California*.[66] Anita Whitney had been convicted under California's Criminal Syndicalism Act for helping organize the Communist party in that state. The law made it a crime to organize or knowingly become a member of any group dedicated to crime, sabotage, or acts of violence in order to bring about social change. The majority of the Court held that the law did not constitute an unreasonable exercise of the state's police power and upheld the conviction.

Brandeis concurred in the opinion because the nature of the appeal made it impossible to inquire into the testimony, which might have allowed him the opportunity to dissent under Holmes's formula of clear and present danger. But because he believed that the Court can only deal with the issues presented directly, he did not dissent; his opinion, however, is as ringing a defense of liberty as anything the more quotable Holmes wrote, and it bears citing at length:

> Those who won our independence believed that the final end of the state was to make men free to develop their faculties; and that in its government the deliberative forces should prevail over the arbitrary. They valued liberty both as an end and as a means. They believed liberty to be the secret of happiness and courage to be the secret of liberty. They believed that freedom to think as you will and to speak as you think are means indispensable to the discovery and spread of political truth; that without free speech and assembly discussion would be futile; that with them, discussion affords ordinarily adequate protection against the dissemination of a noxious doctrine; that the greatest menace to freedom is an inert people; that public discussion is a political duty; and that this should be a fundamental principle of the American government. They recognized the risks to which all human institutions are subject. But they knew that order cannot be secured merely through fear of punishment for its infraction; that it is hazardous to discourage thought, hope and imagination; that fear breeds repression; that repression breeds hate; that hate menaces stable government; that the path of safety lies in the opportunity to discuss freely supposed grievances and proposed remedies; and that the fitting remedy for evil counsels is good ones. Believing in the power of reason as applied through public discussion, they eschewed silence coerced by law—the argument of force in its worst form. Recognizing the occasional tyrannies of governing majorities, they amended the Constitution so that free speech and assembly should be guaranteed.
>
> Fear of serious injury cannot alone justify suppression of free speech and assembly. Men feared witches and burned women. It is the function of speech to free men from the bondage of irrational fears. To justify suppression of free speech there must be reasonable ground to fear that serious evil will result if free speech is practiced. There must be reasonable ground to believe that the danger apprehended is imminent. There must be reasonable ground to believe that the evil to be prevented is a serious one. Every denunciation of existing law

tends in some measure to increase the probability that there will be a violation of it. Condonation of a breach enhances the probability. Expressions of approval add to the probability. Propagation of the criminal state of mind by teaching syndicalism increases it. Advocacy of lawbreaking heightens it still further. But even advocacy of violation, however reprehensible morally, is not a justification for denying free speech where the advocacy falls short of incitement and there is nothing to indicate that the advocacy would be immediately acted on. The wide difference between advocacy and incitement, between preparation and attempt, between assembling and conspiracy, must be borne in mind. In order to support a finding of clear and present danger it must be shown either that immediate serious violence was to be expected or was advocated, or that past conduct furnished reason to believe that such advocacy was then contemplated.

Those who won our independence by revolution were not cowards. They did not fear political change. They did not exalt order at the cost of liberty. To courageous, self-reliant men, with confidence in the power of free and fearless reasoning applied through the processes of popular government, no danger flowing from speech can be deemed clear and present, unless the incidence of the evil apprehended is so imminent that it may befall before there is opportunity for full discussion. If there be time to expose through discussion the falsehood and fallacies, to avert the evil by processes of education, the remedy to be applied is more speech, not enforced silence. Only an emergency can justify repression. Such must be the rule if authority is to be reconciled with freedom. Such, in my opinion, is the command of the Constitution. It is, therefore, always open to Americans to challenge a law abridging free speech and assembly by showing that there was no emergency justifying it.[67]

There are few institutions in this country with the educational impact of the Supreme Court, and there have been few members of that Court so eager to utilize that potential as Brandeis. As a lawyer, he had declared that judges could not be presumed to know the facts; they might know the law, but they would need to be instructed about the facts. As a member of the Court, he used his opinions and dissents to teach his colleagues and, of course, the greater public that law must be related to life.

Despite the success of the "Brandeis brief" in the *Muller* case, the Supreme Court had by no means accepted the full value of such factual demonstrations. The orthodox theory of judicial review held extralegal information to be of dubious value. In practice, aside from Brandeis, few lawyers had had great success with data-laden briefs. In 1916, counsel defending a Washington state statute regulating employment agencies submitted a documented list of grievances to justify the law. Chief Justice White, eyeing the massive brief, commented that he could "compile a brief twice as thick to prove that the legal profession ought to be abolished." [68] In 1923 Mr. Justice Sutherland casually dismissed the enormous amount of background material that Felix Frankfurter laid before the Court in defending the District of Columbia minimum wage law. Sutherland declared the data "proper enough for the consideration of the lawmaking bodies, since their tendency is to establish the desirability or undesirability of the legislation; but they reflect no legitimate light upon its validity." Despite Holmes's comment that the law in the *Muller* case still made good sense as well as good law, a majority of the Court remained unconvinced. [69]

One of the keys, therefore, to understanding Brandeis's role on the Court is to acknowledge the frankly educational function of his writings. It was never enough that he declare his opinion, but he had to explain it. He believed the Court had no business invalidating laws which legislatures, in *their* wisdom, had deemed necessary, except in clear cases of unconstitutionality. When his conservative brethren, however, insisted on interposing their own views of good and bad, he would then go to great lengths to explain just why the legislature had thought the statute in question necessary. [70] The purpose was to put life into the law, to make the Court relevant to the society in which it operated.

Even some of his admirers occasionally wondered whether he overdid it. Roscoe Pound, a great believer in sociological jurisprudence, and Harold Laski both commented that Brandeis should perhaps show greater restraint. "If you could hint to Brandeis," Laski prodded Holmes, "that judicial opinions

aren't to be written in the form of a brief it would be a great
relief to the world. Pound spoke rather strongly as to the advocate in B. being over-prominent in his decisions." Although
Holmes agreed, there was little he could do.[71]

Holmes, in fact, must have been a minor trial of sorts to
Brandeis. Since his days as a law student, Brandeis had admired
Holmes, and had considered him one of the great forces at
work in rejuvenating the law. It had been Holmes who had
once declared that the man of the future in law would be the
"man of statistics and the master of economics," an excellent
prediction of the Brandeis-type lawyer. Yet Holmes despised
facts and economically was extremely naïve. While he admired
Brandeis's ability in economics, he evidenced no desire to par-
take himself. "I prefer the abstract," he wrote. "Brandeis has an
insatiable appetite for facts and . . . I hate them except as pegs
for generalizations, but I admire the gift and wish I had a barn
in which I could store them for use at need. I hope they ma-
nure my soil but they disappear in specie as soon as taken." [72]
Brandeis unsuccessfully tried to get his colleague to see the
light. "Talking with Brandeis yesterday," Holmes reported, "he
drove a harpoon into my midriff by saying that it would be for
the good of my soul to devote my next leisure to the study of
some domain of fact—suggesting the textile industry, which,
after reading many reports &c, I could make living to myself by
a visit to Lawrence. . . . Well, I hate facts." [73] On this occasion, at least, Brandeis had his way, and Holmes packed off a
government report with him on summer vacation; it would be
the last time. The next summer he gratefully confessed that "in
consideration of my age and moral infirmities, [Brandeis] ab-
solved me from facts for the vacation and allowed me my cus-
tomary sport with ideas." [74]

For all their friendship and majestic fighting partnership
against a dead reactionism in law, Holmes and Brandeis differed greatly in their judicial philosophies. Holmes was
Olympian in his aloofness, a liberal, as Laski noted, by nega-
tion. He would not interfere with the rights of legislatures because he would not interfere with the cosmos. Many of his dissents in support of social legislations bear an attitude almost of

disdain. He once described his general philosophy to a friend: "Long ago I decided that I was not God. When a state came in here and wanted to build a slaughter house, I looked at the Constitution and if I couldn't find anything in there that said a state couldn't build a slaughter house I said to myself, if they want to build a slaughter house, God-dammit, let them build it." [75] Despite his reputation as a great liberal, there are many inconsistencies and lapses in his writings; for all of Holmes's devotion to ideas, it is Brandeis who emerges with the more coherent philosophy.

For Brandeis was a liberal by affirmation and championed his causes not out of disinterest, but out of strong beliefs. A Jeffersonian democrat who passionately feared the "curse of bigness," he fought for the rights of states to use their police powers effectively and experimentally in order to preserve a federal system he considered essential for a democratic society. "The attainment of our American ideals," he declared, "is impossible unless the states guard jealously their field of governmental action and perform zealously their appropriate duties." [76]

His devotion to economic independence, to a balanced federal system, and to individual freedom formed a base for the educational work he tried to do on the Court. In a period of transition for the United States into a great industrial power, Brandeis realized that the law would also have to adapt, that it would have to keep pace with the new society. At the same time, he still believed in the old principles and ideals. In his judicial writings, he time and again showed how the old faiths could be adapted to newer times. The heavily documented opinions which so disturbed Harold Laski were essential to providing a guide for American law on how to adjust to new conditions without forsaking old beliefs. At Brandeis's funeral, Dean Acheson noted in the eulogy: "To him truth was less than truth unless it were explained so that people could understand and believe." [77]

Chapter VII

LINCHPIN OF REFORM

It is now three decades since Louis Brandeis died, and our society faces new and different threats both from within and without. In many ways, the "free" life which he exemplified becomes each year more difficult to follow; individuals seem less able to affect the course of events. Mobs and armies and corporations determine policy, while the ranks of our "leaders" are notoriously barren of greatness. Does Brandeis, then, become a figure irrelevant to our times, a curious historical artifact? Or does his life still hold meaning for the society we live in today and will face tomorrow?

Holmes, in his essay on John Marshall, wrote that "a great man represents a great ganglion in the nerves of society, or, to vary the figure, a strategic point in the campaign of history, and part of his greatness consists of his being *there*." [1] Certainly Brandeis and the times went together well. His brilliance and grasp of the nature of a changing economy and society permitted him to understand what was happening; his faith and clear vision in the older democratic ideals, together with immense energy and executive ability, enabled him to rise above the crowd, and to exercise leadership. When law was bent to serve private interests, he became master of law in order that it might serve the public. On the Supreme Court, he articulated the faith that society could regulate the powerful few for the benefit of the powerless many and helped to shape a judicial doctrine to serve the needs of a democratic society in flux.

The "great man" theory, however, makes the man the servant of the times and denies him his own humanity. While we can never know if certain influential figures would have been "great" during other times, we can recognize that some of them had large stature inherent in them. They had certain qualities of mind and spirit, a character, that invites speculation upon their natures. Louis Brandeis was such a man, and, in trying to understand the elements of his greatness, perhaps we can see why he became such an effective reformer.

Certainly, part of his greatness lay in his unflinching character and his determination to be free. He had, as a young man, worked very hard to amass a fortune, so that he would then be able to ignore mundane material concerns. Money as money never interested him—only the freedom that it provided. Similarly, he wanted no bonds other than those voluntarily assumed. At a time in his life when an ambitious lawyer would have welcomed an invitation to run for a sure political office, he refused. Twenty years later, he still shied away from political ties. "I shall be glad," he confided to his brother, "to have no political obligations." [2]

This freedom, while undoubtedly a luxury, also imposed great burdens. He spared few people in his crusades, but he worked himself twice as hard as any of his lieutenants. He immersed himself in the battle and gave all that he had until the fight was won. The greatest sin was indifference, and on that count he would never be found guilty. Once involved in the good cause, "there is nothing for me to do but to follow the trail of evil wherever it extends," he explained. *"Fiat Iustitia.* In the fight against the special interest we shall receive no quarter and may as well make up our minds to give none. It is a hard fight. . . . The chance is none too good. There is a chance—but a chance merely—that the people will now reverse all history and be able to control. The chance is worth taking, because there is nothing left for the self-respecting man to do." [3]

Once on that trail, he proved a persistent and able foe, but not a blind or vindictive one. He saw no use in humiliating his opponents, and unlike many reformers, saw the value of meeting with the "enemy." The successful consolidation of the Boston Gas Company, with its sliding rate scale, resulted because James L. Richards, head of the company, and Brandeis could respect one another. "I believe in compromise," Brandeis said, "if the other fellow is willing to go fifty percent of any hundred percent, but not if he wants to go off in another direction." [4] During the bitter and protracted struggle against the New Haven, Brandeis never once attacked Charles S. Mellen personally; in 1916, before the subcommittee taking testimony on Brandeis's fitness to be a judge, the ex-New Haven head declared that he knew of nothing that could be said against Brandeis.

Brandeis considered character the most important of all virtues, the only one of man's attributes to be admired. He noted approvingly Matthew Arnold's epigram that "life is not a having and a getting, but a being and a becoming." What one did with one's life, how well one used his talents, one's service to his fellowman—these were the only things that mattered. As Paul Freund wrote: "For him achievement and destiny were not measured by size or power or comfort or safety but by character; and character was formed by the process of struggle against adversity, given a fair chance to succeed." [5]

Although he set high standards for his own conduct, he entertained few illusions about the common people. He recognized that most of the time a majority of the populace suffered real or imaginary grievances passively; they had to be organized and inspired to action. "The value of [example] is surely underestimated by even the good people of the world," he wrote to his fiancée. "Most people are like the iron pyrites with which the teachers in physics perform their experiments. They lie powerless—motionless—dormant before the magnet is applied. Then they move wherever they are drawn, and it is a

matter of chance whether it be to the positive or negative pole
to which they march." [6] Indifference, however, was not insu-
perable. "There is in most Americans some spark of idealism,
which can be fanned into a flame. It takes sometimes a divining
rod to find what it is; but when found, and that means often,
when disclosed to the owners, the results are most often
extraordinary." [7]

It is this faith that idealism lay concealed underneath pas-
sivity that marked Brandeis as a democrat of the first rank and
distinguished him from other upper-class reformers of the time.
Despite a common belief that society must change, and that
certain reforms were necessary to improve the condition of the
poor and the working people, many reformers came to the
cause with patrician attitudes bordering on *noblesse oblige*.
They wanted to do things *for* the people and assumed the common people incapable of helping themselves. Frank Munsey exemplified this attitude when he wrote: "It is the work of the
state to think for the people—to teach them how to do, what to
do, and to sustain them in the doing." [8] Brandeis, on the other
hand, firmly believed in the people, not as good followers to be
led (although leadership was required), but as honest men and
women who need only to know and to see the truth in order to
act for themselves. "What I have desired to do," he declared,
"is to make people realize that the most important office, and
the one which all of us can and should fill, is that of private citizen. The duties of the office of private citizen cannot under a
republican form of government be neglected without serious
injury to the public." [9]

His faith in democracy would not be undermined by the
absence of short-term results and dramatic victories; indeed, in
a democracy the wheels of liberty and progress often moved exceedingly slowly. At times, there would be setbacks and defeats;
then, character would be needed, and persistence. Time and
again he urged his colleagues not to be discouraged: "We must
do our best, whatever comes." "Not consistency but persistence
is the jewel." "My faith is great in time—if there be hard
work." [10] Brandeis undoubtedly shared John Jay Chapman's
belief that if one is concerned primarily with moral standards

and character, then "a reverse following a fight for principle
. . . is pure gain. It records the exact state of the cause. It edu-
cates the masses on a gigantic scale. The results of that education are immediately felt." [11]

Perhaps his best statement regarding democratic reform
came in a letter written several years after he had gone on the
Supreme Court:

> Refuse to accept as inevitable any evil in business (e.g., ir-
> regularity of employment). Refuse to tolerate any immoral
> practice (e.g., espionage). But do not believe that you can find
> a universal remedy for evil conditions or immoral practices in
> effecting a fundamental change in society (as by State Social-
> ism). And do not pin too much faith in legislation. Remedial
> institutions are apt to fall under the control of the enemy and
> to become instruments of oppression.

> Seek for betterment within the broad lines of existing in-
> stitutions. Do so by attacking evil *in situ;* and proceed from
> the individual to the general. Remember that progress is nec-
> essarily slow; that remedies are necessarily tentative; that be-
> cause of varying conditions there must be much and constant
> enquiry into facts . . . and much experimentation; and that al-
> ways and everywhere the intellectual, moral and spiritual de-
> velopment of those concerned will remain an essential—and
> the main factor—in real betterment.

> This development of the individual is, thus, both a neces-
> sary means and the end sought. For our objective is the mak-
> ing of men and women who shall be free, self-respecting mem-
> bers of a democracy—and who shall be worthy of respect.
> Improvement in material conditions of the worker and ease
> are the incidents of better conditions—valuable mainly as they
> may ever increase opportunities for development.

> The great developer is responsibility. Hence no remedy
> can be hopeful which does not devolve upon the workers par-
> ticipation in, responsibility for, the conduct of business; and
> their aim should be the eventual assumption of full
> responsibility—as in co-operative enterprises. This participa-
> tion in, and eventual control of, industry is likewise an essen-
> tial of obtaining justice in distributing the fruits of industry.

> But democracy in any sphere is a serious undertaking. It
> substitutes self-restraint for external restraint. It is more diffi-
> cult to maintain than to achieve. It demands continuous sacri-
> fice by the individual and more exigent obedience to the
> moral law than any other form of government. Success in any

democratic undertaking must proceed from the individual. It is possible only where the process of perfecting the individual is pursued. His development is attained mainly in the processes of common living. . . .[12]

As Alvin Johnson noted, Brandeis was a "serenely implacable democrat."

Democracy, however, cannot function in darkness and ignorance. Like Thomas Jefferson, whom he so much admired, Brandeis believed that education undergirded the democratic process. In order to perform their duties as citizens, to vote intelligently, to organize effectively, to fight corruption, to redress grievances, people had to be educated. As early as 1895 he predicted that efforts to curb the trusts would not succeed as long as the average man remained unaware of the evils surrounding large-scale corporate activity.[13] Because of their good nature and forgetfulness, Americans had to be constantly reminded of the work yet to be done. He suggested that the real work of a free press dedicated to reform would be not only informing the public of new evils, but reminding them—educating them—of the old ones as well.[14]

A reform per se, therefore, had little enduring value unless the people understood why it was necessary and how it would function. Therefore, before any meaningful change took place, several steps had to be taken. A good example of the Brandeis method at work was the process leading up to adoption of savings bank life insurance.

Shortly after the New York insurance scandals broke, Brandeis had been asked by policyholders and stockholders to protect their interests in the Equitable Company. While analyzing the abuses uncovered by the Hughes investigation, Brandeis discovered that although the regular policyholders could complain about mismanagement, the working people who bought industrial term insurance with weekly premiums were being bilked left and right. He began to look into the problem, and before long, found himself studying all the different aspects of insurance underwriting.

After educating himself, he now began to educate others, and in a series of speeches helped publicize the numerous abuses attendant to the insurance business; he also devised a plan to correct these evils—inexpensive term insurance and annuities sold through nonprofit savings banks, with rates regulated by the states. Since there would be little additional overhead, no advertising or commissions, and no profit, all of the premiums would be applied to the insurance, with resulting savings in rates and increased value of benefits.

Before publicly unveiling his plan, he sent copies of the article [15] to dozens of people, soliciting their response and their support. This list included civic, religious, business, and labor leaders, as well as colleagues in former battles. With some initial support already garnered, Brandeis now launched a massive campaign to win public acceptance of savings bank insurance. He and Norman White organized the Massachusetts Savings-Bank Insurance League, which ultimately enrolled over 70,000 members. The twin purposes of the League were to exert organized political pressure, and, more importantly, to educate the people as to what it was all about. As Robert Herrick put it, the plan allowed the poor to help themselves; but the poor, and the not-so-poor, had to be made to see this first.

As the pressures on the legislature grew, Brandeis constantly emphasized how important it was to get as many people and groups involved as possible, and then use them to teach others what the issues were. These people were not fools, but intelligent men and women, and Brandeis demanded that they be used as such and treated intelligently. By the time the bill passed in June, 1907, the League had told everybody in the state what it meant and what it could do. In many ways, savings bank life insurance is the archetypical "educational" reform.[16]

Once on the Supreme Court, Brandeis continued in his role as educator; indeed, he believed one of the most important functions of the high court was to educate both fellow judges and the populace at large. His opinions thus pointed out not only the law, but the reasoning and factual background behind the law, whether it was a controversial reform measure or a fine technical point; basic principles had to be expounded. When he learned that more than half of his clerks had returned to law schools as teachers, he remarked with great satisfaction, "Now I have a majority." [17] Faith in democracy sustained his belief that if enough of his followers would work at education in the broadest sense, the good cause would ultimately win out.

Strong character and an unflinching faith in the triumph of democratic processes were rounded out by a brillant analytical mind, one that grasped like a thirsty sponge at every available bit of information. When visitors went to interview him, especially after he had gone on the Court, they frequently reported that they had done nearly all of the talking, while Brandeis had pumped them for all they knew. Not for him abstract speculation or mental dilletantism; he twitted Holmes that improving the mind did not mean rereading familiar classics, but digging into "some domain of unfamiliar fact," and then hunting up every bit of material on it.[18]

Brandeis's ability to gather all types of data, and then probe through, discarding the irrelevant until he had reached the core of the matter, has impressed many scholars. Harold Laski several times marveled at the quality of Brandeis's mental powers and his method of analysis.[19] Felix Frankfurter—admirer, scholar, disciple, lieutenant, and friend—noted that Brandeis defined judgment as "the almost instinctive correlation of a thousand imponderables," and that "he safeguarded and disciplined himself to make sure that he penetrated the imponderables on matters that called for his judgment when the imponderables did not lie on the surface." [20] Paul Freund, a former law clerk who has written very perceptively about Brandeis, states that "he came to each [problem] with a prepared mind, like that of the best scientists, with simple basic ideas, with a determination to unearth and organize a vast disarray of unruly facts, and to impose some order on the disarray by contriving a solution that would be at once just, preventive, and self-motivating." [21]

Freund also notes another characteristic of Brandeis's intellect, one he terms his "morality of mind," which gave a coherence to his labors.[22] Undoubtedly this ingredient set Brandeis apart from other brilliant lawyers of his day, and from the able men with whom he sat on the Court. As a young lawyer, he had insisted not only on being sure that his clients were in the right, but would frequently lecture them on the elements of right in their adversaries' cases. In reform work, he constantly told his colleagues that although their opponent might be in the wrong, he still had some right and rights on his side, and these had to be treated as fairly as those of the community, an attitude that caused a split in the Public Franchise League during the gas consolidation fight. There are few justices of the Court in this century whose opinions hold together with the unity of Brandeis's writings, not alone in legal and technical terms, but in the light of the ethics involved.

This morality of the mind developed from Brandeis's well-thought beliefs regarding the political, social, and economic systems, and permeated his views on them. In an earlier chapter, I suggested that Brandeis's economic thought still attracts us not for its analysis but for its ideology and morality. His faith in democratic processes, and a living law, also reflected that same ethos, and it can be traced directly to his tenacious hold on what he considered the first principles of American life. The unity of his thought rested on his belief that these principles had not been outdated by the country's growth; that they still remained valid and relevant; that these principles had to be sustained if the country were to grow in moral stature as well as in material wealth; and that, therefore, older beliefs would have to be made relevant to new times and new situations. As lawyer, reformer, educator, and judge, he consistently tried to demonstrate that this updating could take place, and he used his full mental abilities to do so. "If we would guide by the light of reason," he wrote, "we must let our minds be bold."

Other men in American history have had strong character, a democratic faith, and a brilliant mind, but few of them have been so effective in such a multiplicity of roles as Brandeis. There have been great lawyers, some of whom became great judges; there have been many reformers. But no one else achieved the pinnacle of professional success, moved so easily and effectively into reform and political circles, and then, in an abrupt and dramatic transition, became one of the handful of intellectual giants among the men who have so far sat on the Supreme Court. The answer, I would suggest, lies in Brandeis's recognition of detail, of the need to set up organizational and administrative frameworks, and of the fact that reform cannot succeed unless properly organized. Not all of his endeavors succeeded; some failed, and others had to overcome numerous setbacks before a triumphant finish. Brandeis learned from past defeats, and in each campaign, he built upon his earlier experience. His organizational techniques, developed layer by layer, nonetheless remained flexible enough to accommodate new interests and new situations.

First of all, he insisted that large numbers of people be involved in his causes for tactical as well as strategic reasons. The rolls of the Savings-Bank Insurance League and the Anti-Merger League numbered into the tens of thousands. In addition to demonstrating wide-scale support, these people provided a personnel pool to which numerous tasks could be assigned—writing letters to representatives, holding public meetings, making personal contacts, and so on. The more involved large numbers of people could be, the more time and energy they would contribute to the cause.

Large numbers also allowed Brandeis to avoid becoming a demagogic manipulator or elitist reformer. Whenever possible, he had other people testify before legislative committees as well as himself, other people make statements for the organization, other people hold positions of authority, so as to divert the spotlight from himself. After the adoption of the sliding rate scale, he told his brother that "I succeeded in running the campaign by putting others on the firing line," while remaining "the man behind." [23] That others stood on the firing line did not mean that Brandeis avoided all controversy or that he retained all the power and control. He recognized that for men to deliver the best they have, they must feel a sense of participation, of obligation, and of authority, and he constantly urged his lieutenants to get as many men as possible into the real work of the organization, and to give them meaningful jobs.[24]

Another reason for the involvement of large numbers can

be found in Brandeis's belief that few men could devote as much time and energy to a cause as he could. Once involved, he concentrated on the task at hand to the utter exclusion of all secondary matters. He had barely returned to his office from a sorely needed rest when he scribbled a typical note to one of his colleagues: "I am just back from my vacation. How is savings bank insurance progressing?" [25] On another occasion, Edward Adler had to caution him against working his followers so hard, since there might be a danger of overworking them.[26] A group of students who had been impressed with Brandeis's campaign for good government in Boston sent a delegation to interview him and find out how they might help. He told them to go down to the City Council meetings and note those items which, after introduction, would be followed up at a later date. They should then divide up the work, and each one go out and read up all that had been written on his particular subject. When the Council brought the item up again, they would know more about their subjects than any of the councilmen and would be listened to with respect and consideration. The students told Brandeis that such a course involved a great deal of work, and they just did not have the time.[27] Only someone with Brandeis's phenomenal memory, or a large group of volunteers, could pursue that particular course successfully.

Brandeis's passion for facts, and more facts, certainly contributed to his effectiveness. He once stated that he tried never to be caught out on a wrong fact, and he seems to have succeeded on that score. He had early realized that lack of information was one of the great deterrents to an aroused public effectively fighting entrenched interests. As long as the public willingly accepted the New Haven's version of its financial condition, for example, they had little chance of reforming the line's management. "The New Haven Primer" effectively tore apart the veil of obfuscation which Mellen had thrown around the road's sinking revenues, and set the stage for the final collapse of the Morgan-sponsored effort at monopolizing New England transportation.

Brandeis shared Woodrow Wilson's belief that publicity would be a potent means of keeping corporations honest. His insistence on uniform accounting procedures so that financial reports would mean the same thing for all corporations was part of that approach. As a young man, he had written that "if the broad sunlight of day could be let in on men's actions, it would purify them as the sun disinfects." [28] In each of his reforms he built up a trenchant publicity apparatus to expose the sins of the enemy, and constantly hailed a free press as one of the safeguards of a well-governed society.[29] Here again, a free press and exposure would serve the function of education, which he deemed essential to a democratic society.

He differed from Wilson, however, in his recognition that the light of day did not last long enough, and when darkness came the old evils frequently returned. But where the muckrakers stopped after exposing bad conditions, Brandeis went on to propose constructive alternatives. If the industrial insurance offered by private companies cost too much and did not offer the workingmen fair compensation, then savings bank life insurance would provide a viable alternate as well as a check on the future activities of the private companies. An attack on railroad management enabled him to promote the idea of scientific management. The deadlock between workers and employers in the garment industry was solved by a "protocol" protecting both sides, and allowing each to air grievances and then work toward solving them. A strike against one of his clients led him to identify the real problem as irregular employment, and he helped establish a new production routine so that workers would no longer suffer long layoffs through no fault of their own. The monopoly of Wall Street called forth a whole set of proposals to break up the money trust and to guard against its remerger.

But, as Max Lerner noted, "most important of all was the will to follow through an idea until it was functioning, and the infinite capacity for pains which saw to the details of an organization." [30] Not only did the evil have to be exposed, not only did an alternative have to be provided, not only did the reform have to be adopted, but then it had to work. The pains he took with the savings bank insurance stretched out for over thirty-five years after the Massachusetts legislature had adopted his proposal. He worked to get the right kind of trustees and staff appointed; to educate the community as to the merits of the plan; to catch minor flaws before they became major ones; to protect the plan from constant attacks by the private companies; to gain new adherents to the program.[31] His follow-through made a success of what his original attack had made possible.

A man's greatness, however, is more than the sum of its parts. One could easily find other elements that made him so effective; one could analyze his writings and break down his philosophy into a well-outlined form. Yet to do so would be a mistake, because Brandeis's life as well as his philosophy formed a unified whole. He had a mind of one piece, in which all of these components meshed and melded together.

Brandeis lived during a time of great stress in American society, an era of transition. Born a few years before Fort Sumter, he died on the eve of Pearl Harbor. During that time enormous changes took place in the United States. A basically rural populace became heterogeneously urban; an essentially agrarian economy developed into the world's most powerful industrial machine; an isolated, provincial country grew into an international colossus. Yet so deep lay his faith in the old verities that he could flexibly adapt them to these new conditions. As a lawyer, he had worked to bring the essential principles of liberty and justice through law into harmony with a new society; as a reformer, he had tried to reconcile industrial necessities with old virtues; as a judge, he was, in Lerner's phrase, "preeminently the jurist of a transitional society, in which change is the dominant, the obtrusive fact." [32]

His appeal lay in that he spoke to both sides, the old and the new. He recognized and welcomed progress, believed in capitalism, and staunchly upheld the rule of law; yet he sustained established moral principles, promoted social justice, and demanded that the law and the real world be brought into a just harmony. Those lost in a transitional society normally flounder around for some stable rock, some identification with the known. In the early twentieth century, Brandeis's social thought provided that stability to many men and women who recognized that their old world was fast disappearing and did not know what the new world would bring.

This sense of floundering affected not only those who yearned for an older, idyllic America, such as a Woodrow Wilson or a Josephus Daniels, but also those who on the surface, at least, professed unbounded optimism and confidence in the newer society, such as a Theodore Roosevelt or a Herbert Croly. In the ranks of reformers, at least, Brandeis had few enemies. Even those who disagreed with his philosophy never questioned his integrity or his faith in American principles. Roosevelt, for instance, despised Woodrow Wilson, yet held great respect for Brandeis; so too did the Pinchot brothers, Walter Lippmann, and others who rallied to the banners of the New Nationalism in 1912.

This respect from all parts of the progressive movement may be crucial in understanding that phenomenal burst of reforming zeal prior to World War I. There have been many theories set forth by a number of historians as to the nature of progressive reform and the forces that called it into being. Progressivism has been described as a response to industrialism, a search for order, and its motive forces have been variously placed in the middle classes, the upper class, the lower class, and a displaced élite.[33] All of these theories have too many kernels of truth in them to be dismissed out of hand, yet each also has too many inconsistencies to be accepted fully. In order to understand progressivism, as well as the major actors who marched across the stage of reform, one must somehow try to impose some sort of historical framework upon the period, and still remain flexible enough to accommodate its numerous idiosyncrasies.

No one hypothesis can do justice to a movement so variegated as was progressivism. When both Woodrow Wilson and Theodore Roosevelt can be described as "the" archetypical progressive, it becomes extremely frustrating to delineate a rational framework in which the two can exist in peace and harmony, much less brotherhood. Even taking certain aspects of progressivism, such as educational reform, the landscape becomes too crowded with groups and figures to allow ordering.³⁴

It is necessary, then, to treat progressivism on its own terms and expand historical parameters to allow the various life-forms some room for examination. There is general agreement that the progressive impulse took place during a transitional period in American society, in which the motor force of change was the rapid expansion and industrialization of the economy. This industrialization touched upon numerous facets of life, and different groups, depending upon how they were affected, responded in different ways. One group, appalled by the waste of natural resources, became conservationists. Another, frightened by the growth of large private corporations with huge economic and political power, turned to antitrust activities. Still others, grieved by the terrible toll exacted by factory demands upon human life, turned to a number of social reforms, such as factory inspection, wage and hours laws, moral uplift, and other methods of regeneration. The list could be expanded still further, to include those whose prime concerns were urban planning, good government, education, immigration restriction, food, meat, and drug laws, prohibition, and so on.

While it is true that many progressives belonged to a number of these groups, for the most part each faction operated discretely, and frequently at odds with fellow reformers. Two men who could support factory reform at one meeting might turn into bitter antagonists when it came to the problem of prohibition. Civil libertarians and prohibitionists might join together to battle for conservation. Conservation itself can be construed as a broad blanket covering a number of uneasy bedfellows. To secure the necessary legislation for industrial education, a loose alliance of social workers, the American Federation of Labor, the National Association of Manufacturers, the Chamber of Commerce, and the Grange found common ground in the National Society for the Promotion of Industrial Education, and promptly disbanded with the passage of the Smith-Hughes Act in 1917. The history of the Federal Reserve Act also shows how antagonistic groups could unite on common, though narrow, grounds.

Holding these reforms together were men like Louis Brandeis and women like Jane Addams, figures who might properly be entitled "linchpins of reform." Through their own efforts in a number of reforms, and the respect they won from all groups, they were able to move easily from one faction to another, helping to create new alliances for each issue. Woodrow Wilson, Robert LaFollette, and Theodore Roosevelt all worked at some time together with Brandeis, and each recognized how important a political ally he could be. For those committed to their own efforts to improve the world, and who may have considered the differences between the New Freedom and the New Nationalism minimal, the example of someone like Brandeis carried weight.

In an earlier chapter I referred to Brandeis as a "reformer of reformers," and by this meant two things. In one way, we can look at the large number of causes with which he allied himself—good government, traction reform, improvement of mental institutions, education, conservation, wage and hour regulation, scientific management, control of public and semi-public corporations and utilities, modernization of legal codes, Zionism, antitrust work, monetary reform—the list seems endless. In another sense, we can refer to the standing and respect that he held among the leaders of these movements, many of whom he worked with on numerous occasions—Morris L. Cooke, Ray Stannard Baker, Rudolf Spreckels, Frederick Taylor, Frank Galbraith, Abraham Flexner, James R. Garfield, Charles Evans Hughes, Norman Hapgood, Joseph B. Eastman (whom he trained), Herbert Hoover, Meyer London, Jane Addams, Felix Frankfurter, Roscoe Pound, the Pinchot brothers, Clarence Darrow, Robert M. LaFollette, Woodrow Wilson, Theodore Roosevelt, Samuel Gompers, Lincoln Steffens, Stephen Wise, Florence Kelley, Josephine Goldmark, the Kellogg brothers, Frederick C. Howe, George Rublee, Thomas Walsh, Samuel Untermyer, George W. Norris, Herbert Croly, Oliver Wendell Holmes, Morris Hillquit, Walter Lippmann, John Graham Brooks—the list could go on for pages.

By moving among such groups and peoples, Brandeis and

others like him—a handful at most—helped hold together that amorphous mixture of reformers and ideas and uplift we have termed progressivism. Reform, after all, is not primarily a social or institutional phenomenon, but the collective result of many individual efforts.

Louis Brandeis had become a patron saint to reformers of many shades by the time of his death, on October 5, 1941. His ideals, his character, his faith in democracy, his effectiveness, his own example of a "free life" had inspired men and women for more than four decades. At his funeral, Dean Acheson spoke not only for the law clerks, but for all who had known him: "Throughout these years we have brought him all of our problems and all our troubles, and he had time for all of us. A question, a comment, and the difficulties began to disappear; the dross and shoddy began to appear for what it was, and we wondered why the matter had ever seemed difficult. . . . [We] saw in action his burning faith that the verities to which men had clung through the ages were verities; that evil never could be good; that falsehood was not truth, not even if all the ingenuity of science reiterated it in waves that encircled the earth. . . . But to him truth was less than truth unless it was expounded so that people could understand and believe. During these years of retreat from reason, his faith in the human mind and in the will and capacity of people to understand and grasp the truth never wavered or tired. In a time of moral and intellectual anarchy and frustration, he handed on the great tradition of faith in the mind and spirit of man which is the faith of the prophets and poets, of Socrates, of Lincoln." [35]

His friend and disciple, Mr. Justice Frankfurter, then compared him to Bunyan's Mr. Valiant-for-Truth, and noted that "the quality of the life to which we pay reverence, Hebrew prophets have foretold with accuracy:

'The law of truth was in his mouth, and unrighteousness was not found in his lips; he walked with me in peace and equity, and did turn many away from iniquity.'

'Behold, a king shall reign in righteousness, and princes shall rule in judgment.'

'And a man shall be as a hiding place from the wind, and a covert from the tempest; as rivers of water in a dry place, as the shadow of a great rock in a weary land.'

NOTES
BIBLIOGRAPHY
INDEX

NOTES

Chapter I

1. *Reminiscences of Frederika Dembitz Brandeis,* trans. Alice G. Brandeis (privately printed, 1943), 33.

2. Arthur Mann, *Yankee Reformers in the Urban Age* (New York, 1966 ed.), 11, 22.

3. *Ibid.,* 20.

4. Louis D. Brandeis, "The Harvard Law School," 1 *Green Bag* 10 (1889). The social and intellectual currents at the School may be considered part and parcel of those in the larger Boston society.

5. Louis Brandeis (LDB) to Otto Wehle, March 12 and November 12, 1876, in the Papers of Louis Dembitz Brandeis, University of Louisville Law Library, Louisville, Kentucky.

6. For details, see Alpheus Thomas Mason, *Brandeis—A Free Man's Life* (New York, 1946), 64–67; see also LDB to Alfred Brandeis, March 21, 1887, Brandeis MSS.

7. See, for example, LDB to Alfred Brandeis, June 28, 1878, and LDB to Alice Goldmark, October 13, 1890, both in possession of Mrs. Elizabeth Brandeis Raushenbush, Madison, Wisconsin.

8. Richard M. Abrams, *Conservatism in a Progressive Era* (Cambridge, Mass., 1964), 4, 11; see also James Lord Bryce, *The American*

Commonwealth, 2 vols. (London and New York, 1888), I, 515, and Alice Felt Tyler, *Freedom's Ferment* (Minneapolis, Minn., 1944), *passim.*

9. LDB to Henry Morgenthau, Sr., December 5, 1906, Archives of the Division of Savings Bank Life Insurance, Boston, Massachusetts.

10. Richard M. Abrams, "Brandeis and the New Haven-Boston & Maine Merger Battle Revisited," *Business History Review,* XXXVI (1962), 408–30.

11. Paul Freund, "Mr. Justice Brandeis," in A. Dunham and P. B. Kurland, eds., *Mr. Justice* (Chicago, 1956), 99; see especially LDB to Robert W. Bruere, February 25, 1922, Brandeis MSS.

12. LDB to Adolph Brandeis, November 21, 1889, Brandeis MSS. LDB remained uneasy, however, with George's radical views on property.

13. The numerous letters in the Savings Bank Archives are filled with directives from LDB to his lieutenants, stressing the theme that the reform could only succeed if it had the backing of the people, and therefore their participation was vital.

14. LDB to Alfred Brandeis, May 1, 1910; LDB, speech to Boston Public School Association, November 15, 1904; both in Brandeis MSS. Interview with Mrs. E. B. Raushenbush, July 17, 1969.

15. An excellent article exploring this attitude is George Wilson Pierson, "The Obstinate Concept of New England: A Study of Denudation," *New England Quarterly,* XXVIII (1955), 3–17.

16. LDB to Policyholders . . . , July 22, 1905, copy courtesy of Mrs. E. B. Raushenbush. The only available study of this reform is Alpheus T. Mason, *The Brandeis Way* (Princeton, 1938).

17. LDB to Robert L. O'Brien, March 30, 1907, Savings Bank Insurance Archives.

18. Abrams, "Brandeis and the New Haven," *passim.*

19. Louis D. Brandeis, *Other People's Money, and How the Bankers Use It* (New York, 1914).

20. It should be noted that their accomplishments were in fields vitally useful and necessary to the growth and prosperity of the Commonwealth; if they had excelled in less useful tasks, the public approbation would have been commensurately less.

21. See Charles Francis Adams, Jr., and Henry Adams, *Chapters of Erie, and Other Essays* (Boston, 1871), and *The Education of Henry*

Adams (Boston, 1918). The Adams family had never been too happy even with the financiers of State Street, and the new Wall Street breed was totally beyond their ken.

22. Abrams, *Conservatism in a Progressive Era,* 28.

23. Frederic C. Jaher, "Aristocracy in America: The Case of the Boston Brahmins," unpublished manuscript courtesy of Professor Jaher; a briefer version appears in F. C. Jaher, ed., *The Age of Industrialism* (New York, 1968).

24. Mann, *op. cit.,* 7.

25. Irving Katz, "Henry Lee Higginson vs. Louis Dembitz Brandeis: A Collision Between Tradition and Reform," *New England Quarterly,* XLI (1968), 72, 74.

26. Jaher, *op. cit.,* 78. The fact that LDB had such extensive connections with Harvard no doubt facilitated his entry into proper circles.

27. Interview with Mrs. E. B. Raushenbush, July 17, 1969.

28. Of course, by then he had become the leader of American Zionists, and despite his assimilationist beliefs, the bigots condemned him along with every other Jew. To orthodox Jews, LDB hardly qualified as a coreligionist, and to the best of my knowledge, he never practiced any of the ritual requirements of the faith. He did, however, contribute regularly to Jewish charities in Boston, and his attitude was familiar and acceptable to many Reform and assimilation-minded Jews. For further comment, see Chapter 5.

29. See, for example, James K. Hosmer, *The Story of the Jews* (New York, 1885).

30. *Democracy* (New York, 1880). In contrast to his earlier admiration of Jews, Adams later succumbed, along with many other Brahmins, to a vicious anti-Semitism. "His world is dead," he later wrote of himself and his kind. "Not a Polish Jew fresh from Warsaw or Cracow— not a furtive Yacoob or Ysaac still reeking of the Ghetto, snarling a weird Yiddish to the officers of the customs—but had a keener instinct, an intenser energy, and a freer hand than he—American of Americans, with Heaven knows how many Puritans and Patriots behind him, and an education that had cost a civil war." (*Education of Henry Adams,* 238.)

31. Much of the above is drawn from Barbara M. Solomon, *Ancestors and Immigrants: A Changing New England Tradition* (Cambridge, Mass., 1956).

32. An excellent essay on Rabbi Schindler is in Mann, *op. cit.*, Ch. 3.

33. *Boston American,* July 4, 1915.

34. For the ideological differences between American and European Zionists, see Chapter 5.

35. Katz, *op. cit.,* 75.

36. Higginson, of course, is considered only as archetypical of those Bostonians who had retreated into caste-consciousness.

37. Louis D. Brandeis, "Our New Peonage: Discretionary Pensions," *The Independent,* LXXIII (July 25, 1912), 187. There are many examples of this sentiment in his writings; see, among others: "Business—the New Profession," *System,* XXII (October, 1912), 365–69; testimony before the United States Industrial Commission in Senate Document 415, 64th Cong., 1st Sess., XIX, 991–1011 (April 16, 1914); testimony before House Committee on Interstate and Foreign Commerce, 64th Cong., 1st Sess., *Hearings on Regulation of Prices,* 198–243 (January 9, 1915); Alfred Lief, ed., *The Social and Economic Views of Mr. Justice Brandeis* (New York, 1930), *passim.*

38. See Chapter 4.

39. During the several weeks of hearings regarding his appointment to the Supreme Court in 1916, despite many allegations of irregular and unethical behavior, not one charge of misconduct could be substantiated. See *Hearings . . . ,* Senate Document 409, 64th Cong., 1st Sess. (1916) (hereafter cited as *Nom. Hearings*).

40. See Felix Frankfurter to Arthur M. Schlesinger, June 18, 1963, reprinted in Max Freedman, ed., *Roosevelt & Frankfurter: Their Correspondence, 1928–1945* (Boston, 1967), 24–26.

41. When Charles S. Mellen supposedly sold the New Haven's holdings in the B & M to a John Billard, LDB at first was willing to accept this as true. After some investigation, however, LDB characterized the sale as fraudulent. Higginson then declared that Brandeis's charge merely proved that LDB himself was accustomed to lying. According to Abrams, Higginson was in a position to know the real facts concerning the phony transaction. (Abrams, *Conservatism in a Progressive Era,* 205 n.)

Chapter II

1. Samuel J. Konefsky, *The Legacy of Holmes and Brandeis: A Study in the Influence of Ideas* (New York, 1961), 278 n.

2. Figures on growth and change in the United States can be found in *Historical Statistics of the United States* (Washington, 1960), *passim*.

3. James Willard Hurst, *The Growth of American Law: The Law Makers* (Boston, 1950), 339.

4. *Ibid.,* 345.

5. Oliver Wendell Holmes, Jr., "The Path of the Law," *Collected Legal Papers* (New York, 1920), 187.

6. For a study of the growth of a corporate law firm, see Robert T. Swaine, *The Cravath Firm* (New York, 1946), 1, *passim*.

7. *Felix Frankfurter Reminisces* (New York, 1960), 128.

8. Both cited in David W. Levy, "The Lawyer as Judge: Brandeis' View of the Legal Profession," 22 *Oklahoma Law Review* 374, 377–78 (1969). While Professor Levy and I both share many views regarding LDB's legal philosophy, the reader will discern a number of differences in outlook and interpretation.

9. Arnold M. Paul, *Conservative Crisis and the Rule of Law: Attitudes of Bar and Bench, 1887–1895* (Ithaca, 1960), 65.

10. The tenets of this creed are examined in *ibid.;* Robert G. McCloskey, *American Conservatism in the Age of Enterprise, 1865–1910* (New York, 1964); and Sidney Fine, *Laissez-Faire and the General Welfare State* (Ann Arbor, Mich., 1956), 160.

11. Fine, *op. cit.*

12. In *Ex parte Kuback,* 85 Cal. 274 (1890), the only authority cited was Thomas McIntyre Cooley's book, *A Treatise on the Constitutional Limitations Which Rest Upon the Legislative Power of the States of the American Union* (Boston, 1868).

13. Fine, *op. cit.,* 160–62; Roscoe Pound, "Liberty of Contract," 18 *Yale Law Journal* 454 (1909).

14. *United States v. E. C. Knight,* 156 U.S. I (1895); *Pollack v. Farmers' Loan and Trust Company,* 158 U.S. 601 (1895).

15. Paul, *op. cit.,* 2.

16. *Munn v. Illinois,* 94 U.S. 113, 136 (1876).

17. *Powell v. Pennsylvania,* 127 U.S. 678 (1888); *Allgeyer v. Louisiana,* 165 U.S. 578 (1897). Field is not the only judge to work to change his dissent into majority opinion. Both LDB and Holmes originally were in a minority in their view of the protection of speech and the power of states to regulate hours and wages, yet by the time LDB left the Court in 1939, much of the earlier dissent was incorporated into accepted doctrine.

18. Paul, *op. cit.,* 63–64; McCloskey, *op. cit.,* Ch. 4.

19. *In re Jacobs,* 98 N.Y. 98 (1885); *Ritchie v. People,* 155 Ill. 98 (1895); *State v. Goodwill,* 33 W. Va. 179 (1889).

20. *Farmers' Loan & Trust Co. v. Northern Pacific R.R. Co.,* 60 Fed. 803 (1894).

21. Fine, *op. cit.,* 139. N.B.: The use of the word "conservative" here is obviously different from the way LDB used it.

22. Paul, *op. cit.,* 164.

23. Cooley, *op. cit.* Cooley's original emphasis was greatly distorted by judges and lawyers who seized upon one section of the work. See Alan Jones, "Thomas M. Cooley and 'Laissez-Faire Constitutionalism': A Reconsideration," *Journal of American History,* LIII (1967), 751–71.

24. According to one legal historian, Dembitz's *Land Titles in the United States,* 2 vols. (St. Paul, 1885), is an intellectual tour de force, in which the author took a number of pieces in a complex subject and organized them so even a layman could understand the topic.

25. LDB to Otto Wehle, March 12, 1876, Brandeis MSS; LDB to Amy Brandeis Wehle, January 20, 1877, in the Louis B. Wehle Papers, Franklin D. Roosevelt Library, Hyde Park, New York.

26. LDB to Samuel D. Warren, cited in Alpheus T. Mason, *Brandeis —A Free Man's Life* (New York, 1946), 54–55.

27. LDB to Alfred Brandeis, March 21, 1887, in author's possession; see also LDB to Amy Brandeis Wehle, January 2, 1881, Brandeis MSS.

28. An account of Brandeis's practice is Edward F. McClennan's "Louis D. Brandeis as a Lawyer," 33 *Massachusetts Law Quarterly* 1

(1948). This article was originally prepared as a memorandum to assist A. T. Mason in writing Brandeis's biography.

29. Memorandum, "What the practice of law includes," Brandeis MSS.

30. LDB to William H. Dunbar, February 2, 1893, in Felix Frankfurter Papers, Library of Congress, Washington, D.C.

31. LDB to Dunbar, August 19, 1896, cited in McClennan, *op. cit.,* 15–16.

32. Hurst, *op. cit.,* 311; Mason, *op. cit.,* 640.

33. Paul, *op. cit.,* 50–60; Morton White, *Social Thought in America: The Revolt against Formalism* (Boston, 1957), Ch. 5.

34. Oliver Wendell Holmes, Jr., *The Common Law* (Boston, 1881), 1.

35. See, for example, his classic dissent in *Lochner v. New York,* 198 U.S. 45, 74 (1905).

36. 24 *Chicago Legal News* 410 (1892), and 26 *American Law Review* 849 (1892), both cited in Paul, *op. cit.* 44, 53–54.

37. LDB to John Hinkley, July 20, 1905, Brandeis MSS.

38. LDB, "The Living Law," 10 *Illinois Law Review* 461, 463–64 (1916). This speech, given before the Chicago Bar Association on January 3, 1916, just prior to his nomination to the bench, summed up Brandeis's philosophy about the law and the role of the lawyer. It is reprinted in Osmond K. Fraenkel, *The Curse of Bigness: Miscellaneous Papers of Louis D. Brandeis* (New York, 1934).

39. *Ibid.,* 463.

40. LDB to Norman Hapgood, April 9, 1912, Brandeis MSS.

41. *Ritchie v. People,* 155 Ill. 98 (1895); *Ritchie v. Wageman,* 244 Ill. 508 (1910). LDB appeared as counsel for the state in the latter case.

42. LDB, "The Living Law," 465. By the second Ritchie case, the Court had the precedent of the Muller case to influence its thinking.

43. Statement to Massachusetts Joint Legislative Committee on Liquor Law, February 27, 1891, in Scrapbook I, Brandeis MSS.

44. Statement to House Committee on Patents, May 15, 1912, cited in Alfred Lief, ed., *The Brandeis Guide to the Modern World* (Boston, 1941), 165.

45. Dissenting opinion in *DiSanto v. Pennsylvania,* 273 U.S. 34, 37 (1927), at 43.

46. Paul Freund, "Mr. Justice Brandeis," in Allison Dunham and Philip Kurland, eds., *Mr. Justice* (Chicago, 1956), 97–121, at 102.

47. McClennan, *op. cit.,* 22–23; in the 1880s, LDB had gone to England to negotiate patent rights on a bleacher for the Warren paper interests.

48. LDB, "The Living Law," 470.

49. This irony is well brought out in Mason, *op. cit.,* Chs. 30, 31.

50. *Ibid.,* 145–46.

51. McClennan, *op. cit.,* 26.

52. Hurst, *op. cit.,* 354.

53. LDB to John Holmes, June 20, 1905, Brandeis MSS; Boston *Herald,* June 20, 1905.

54. "The Opportunity in the Law," 39 *American Law Review,* 555, 559, (1905), originally delivered as a talk to the Harvard Ethical Society, May 4, 1905.

55. Edward A. Filene, "Louis D. Brandeis As We Know Him," Boston *Post,* July 14, 1915.

56. LDB to Charles Palen Hall, July 13, 1906, Brandeis MSS.

57. The phrase was used by Holmes to describe Brandeis; Holmes to Felix Frankfurter, August 14, 1916, cited in Alexander M. Bickel, *The Unpublished Opinions of Mr. Justice Brandeis* (Cambridge, Mass., 1957), 222.

58. LDB to E. Louise Malloch, November 4, 1907, Brandeis MSS; LDB paid the firm because he constantly drew upon the specialized talents he had built up there. McClennan notes that at one time he paid the firm $25,000 for its services (including his) in a public cause.

59. *Current Literature* (March, 1911), cited in Lief, *op. cit.,* 38.

60. *Ibid.*

61. Mason, *op. cit.,* 232–37.

62. McClennan, *op. cit.,* 21.

63. Levy, *op. cit.,* 389.

64. LDB, "The Living Law," 470.

65. *Ibid.*

66. For his feelings about the school, see LDB, "The Harvard Law School," 1 *Green Bag* 10 (1889), and LDB to Thomas F. Bayard, May 17, 1890, in Thomas Francis Bayard Papers, Library of Congress.

67. LDB to Christopher Columbus Langdell, December 30, 1889, in Scrapbook I, Brandeis MSS; LDB to Langdell, April 10, 1893, to Charles W. Eliot, April 25, 1893, March 30, 1894, in Charles W. Eliot Papers, Harvard University Archives, Cambridge, Massachusetts.

68. LDB to Norman Hapgood, July 30, 1912, Brandeis MSS.

69. Quoting C. F. Henderson, "The Living Law," 470.

70. Homer Albers, Dean of the Boston University Law School, quoted in Konefsky, *op. cit.,* 69.

71. LDB to officers of local bar associations, April, 1900, Brandeis MSS.

72. LDB, "The Living Law," 470.

73. *Muller v. Oregon,* 208 U.S. 412 (1908).

74. The brief, together with the Court's decision, can be found in a Consumer League publication, *Women in Industry. . . .* (New York, 1908).

75. The best account of the case, and of the work that went into it, is Chapter 13 of Josephine Goldmark, *Impatient Crusader: Florence Kelley's Life Story* (Urbana, Ill., 1953).

76. *Lochner v. New York,* 198 U.S. 45 (1905).

77. Goldmark, *op. cit.,* 154.

78. Mason, *op. cit.,* 248–49.

79. Cited in Konefsky, *op. cit.,* 87–8; see also Harold J. Laski to Oliver Wendell Holmes, Jr., March 26, 1932, in Mark A. DeWolfe Howe, ed., *Holmes–Laski Letters* (Cambridge, Mass., 1953), II, 1,372.

80. Interestingly, the women's liberation movement has spawned a backlash regarding protective legislation. Some of the more militant fem-

inists oppose any law that distinguishes between sexes, and they consider the *Muller* brief an example of chauvinistic paternalism. See Kate Millett, *Sexual Politics* (New York, 1970), 88. Any careful reading of the brief indicates that: (a) LDB drew upon the most recent knowledge of that era; and (b) he was trying, through remedial legislation, to eliminate the exploitation of women in industry. The decision of the Court was no doubt paternalistic, but it is inane to condemn men of good will because they were not prophetic enough six decades ago to realize that women's lib might come along. LDB, by the way, did support women's suffrage.

81.   *Muller* acknowledged the legitimacy of regulation of hours, although the concept would be challenged again in the courts. LDB defended the Illinois law again in *People v. Eldering*, 254 Ill. 579 (1912), and also successfully defended an Ohio law regulating hours for women, *Hawley v. Walker*, 232 U.S. 718 (1914). Minimum wage regulation was defended by Brandeis before the Supreme Court, with a divided bench sustaining the legislation, *Stettler v. O'Hara*, 243 U.S. 629 (1916), but the victory was illusory. In 1923, federal wage legislation was struck down in *Adkins v. Children's Hospital*, 261 U.S. 525, with Sutherland citing *Lochner* as a precedent. In 1936 the Court struck down a state statute in *Morehead v. New York ex rel. Tipaldo*, 298 U.S. 587. Finally in 1937, by a five to four vote, the Court validated the concept of minimum wage legislation in *West Coast Hotel Co. v. Parrish*, 300 U.S. 379; LDB, then in his twenty-first year on the Court, had lived to see the law and social needs come together.

Chapter III

1.   *Wealth of Nations,* quoted in John Kenneth Galbraith, *American Capitalism* (Boston, 1956 ed.), 14.

2.   Gabriel Kolko, *The Triumph of Conservatism* (New York, 1963), 18–19.

3.   House of Representatives, Committee on the Judiciary, *Hearings . . . on Study of Monopoly Power,* 81st Cong., 1st Sess. (Washington, 1949), 103; Abraham Berglund, *The United States Steel Corporation* (New York, 1907), 78.

4.   Henry Demarest Lloyd, *Wealth against Commonwealth* (New York, 1894); Matthew Josephson, *The Robber Barons* (New York, 1934). A partial corrective is Allan Nevins, *John D. Rockefeller* (New York, 1940, two vols.) and its subsequent revision.

5.   Kolko, *op. cit.,* 13.

6.   Irvin G. Wyllie, *The Self-Made Man in America* (New Brunswick, N.J., 1954), *passim*. Despite a great deal of evidence that many of the great business leaders had not risen from rags to riches, a sufficient number had done so to sustain the belief in the self-made man.

7.   John A. Garraty, *The New Commonwealth, 1877–1890* (New York, 1968), 31.

8.   Edward C. Kirkland, *Dream and Thought in the Business Community, 1860–1900* (Ithaca, N.Y., 1956), 121; Sidney Fine, *Laissez-Faire and the General Welfare State* (Ann Arbor, Mich., 1956), 30.

9.   Fine, *op. cit.*, 111.

10.   Quoted in Wyllie, *op. cit.*, 167.

11.   Arthur Jerome Eddy, *The New Competition* (Chicago, 1916, 5th ed.). See also Charles R. VanHise, *Concentration and Control* (New York, 1912), and Herbert Croly, *The Promise of American Life* (New York, 1909).

12.   Arthur P. Dudden, "Men Against Monopoly: the Prelude to Trust-Busting," *Journal of the History of Ideas*, XVIII (1957), 587, 589.

13.   Henry George, *Progress and Poverty* (New York, 1879). See also Charles Barker, *Henry George* (New York, 1955).

14.   Arthur Mann, *Yankee Reformers in the Urban Age* (New York, 1966 ed.), Ch. 6.

15.   J. Leonard Bates, "Fulfilling American Democracy: the Conservation Movement, 1907 to 1921," *Mississippi Valley Historical Review*, XLIV (1957), 31.

16.   Mann, *op. cit.*, 104–5.

17.   LDB to Alfred Brandeis, July 28, 1904, Brandeis MSS.

18.   Conversation with Alfred Lief, April 15, 1934, in A. Lief, ed., *The Brandeis Guide to the Modern World* (Boston, 1941), 116.

19.   LDB to Norman Hapgood, September 25, 1911, Brandeis MSS.

20.   Senate Committee on Interstate Commerce, *Hearings on Control of Corporations, Persons, and Firms Engaged in Interstate Commerce*, 62nd Cong., 2nd Sess. (Washington, 1911).

21.   New York, 1914.

22.   Brandeis, "Our New Peonage: Discretionary Pensions," *The Independent*, LXXIII (July 25, 1912), 187.

23.   Senate Committee on Interstate Commerce, *op. cit.*

24.   Brandeis, "Cutthroat Prices: The Competition That Kills," *Harper's Weekly*, LVIII (November 15, 1913), 10–12.

25.   Quoted in Lief, *op. cit.*, 124.

26.   Testimony before United States Commission on Industrial Relations, printed in O. K. Fraenkel, ed., *The Curse of Bigness: Miscellaneous Papers of Louis D. Brandeis* (New York, 1934), 81.

27.   Brandeis, "Life Insurance: The Abuses and the Remedies," in *Business—A Profession* (Boston, 1914), 112.

28.   Brandeis, "Shall We Abandon the Policy of Competition?" *Case and Comment*, XVIII, 494 (1912), reprinted in Fraenkel, *op. cit.*, 105.

29.   Brandeis, "Trusts, Efficiency, and the New Party," *Collier's Weekly*, XLIX (September 14, 1912), 14.

30.   Conversation with Lief, April 15, 1934, in Lief, *op. cit.*, 70.

31.   See below, Chapter 5.

32.   Senate Committee on Interstate Commerce, *op. cit.*

33.   See next chapter.

34.   Brandeis, "The New England Transportation Monopoly," in *Business—A Profession*, 275–76. This sentiment is expressed in many places, among them an interview in the Boston *Journal*, December 13, 1912; Senate Committee on Interstate Commerce, *op. cit.;* and the article in *Collier's* cited in note 29.

35.   LDB to Harold Laski, September 21, 1921, in Harold Laski Papers, Law Library of Yale University, New Haven, Connecticut.

36.   LDB to Lorin Deland, February 9, 1895, in Lief, *op. cit.*, 161.

37.   Statement on subway bill, April 14, 1901, Brandeis MSS.

38.   See his statement to House Committee on Interstate Commerce, *Hearings on Regulation of Prices*, 64th Cong., 1st Sess. (Washington, 1915).

39.   LDB to Norman Hapgood, May 28, 1906; LDB to Lawrence Abbott, May 26, 1907; both in Brandeis MSS. The sliding-scale system

failed during the First World War, when it proved too inflexible in a period of rapidly rising production costs. The system assumed stable times, in which problems could be slowly but surely eliminated and service improved. It had not assumed that extraordinary stress would throw the entire system out of kilter.

40.   LDB to Louis F. Buff, February 3, 1908, Brandeis MSS.

41.   Alfred D. Chandler, Jr., "The Beginnings of 'Big Business' in American Industry," *Business History Review*, XXXIII (1959), 1–31.

42.   Alfred Lubell and Eloy R. Mestre, "The Demand Function and Economic Concentration," MS courtesy of Professor Lubell.

43.   Galbraith, *op. cit.*, 33.

44.   There are, of course, exceptions to this statement, of which the most obvious is that of United States Steel from 1920 to the end of the Second World War. However, as the Temporary National Economic Commission hearings showed, this was due to the fear that attempts to increase U.S. Steel's efficiency might so increase its share of the market as to bring down an antitrust suit on its head. At the same time, Bethlehem Steel under Charles Schwab demonstrated just how efficient and innovative a large company could be.

45.   Galbraith, *op. cit.*, 90. An excellent example is the coal industry which is as close as we can get to a purely competitive model in industry. There have been no major innovations in years, and the industry has been declining as a result of pressures from gas and oil, both products of oligopolistic industries. The typical coal operator works on a thin margin of profit, has no room for innovation, and cannot seem to get together with other operators to develop new uses for his product.

46.   Joel B. Dirlam and Alfred E. Kahn, *Fair Competition: The Law and Economics of Antitrust Policy* (Ithaca, 1954), 11.

47.   See, among others, J. M. Clark, "Toward a Concept of Workable Competition," *American Economic Review*, XXX (1940), 241–56; Edward H. Chamberlain, *The Theory of Monopolistic Competition* (Cambridge, 1948, 6th ed); and for a more popular exposition, David E. Lilienthal, *Big Business: A New Era* (New York, 1952).

Chapter IV

1.   Arthur S. Link, *Wilson* (Princeton, 1947–   , five vols. to date), I, 489; II, 95.

2. See, for example, Franklin K. Lane to Francis G. Newlands, October 28, 1912, in A. W. Lane and L. H. Hall, eds., *The Letters of Franklin K. Lane, Personal and Political* (Boston, 1922), 109; Jerome J. Wilbur to Frank Trumbull, December 16, 1913, in the Frank Arthur Vanderlip Papers, Columbia University, New York; Woodrow Wilson to Charles A. Culberson, May 5, 1916, in *Nom. Hearings,* II, 6.

3. William Diamond, *The Economic Thought of Woodrow Wilson* (Baltimore, 1943), 21–22, 37.

4. Link, *op. cit.,* I, 111, 119; Woodrow Wilson, *A History of the American People* (New York, 1902), V, 167.

5. Richard Hofstadter, *The Age of Reform* (New York, 1955), 22–223; see also his essay on Wilson in *The American Political Tradition* (New York, 1958 ed.), Ch. 10. A similar sentiment is in T. W. Gregory to Josephus Daniels, February 19, 1924, in the Thomas W. Gregory Papers, Library of Congress, Washington, D.C.

6. Ray Stannard Baker and William E. Dodd, eds., *The Public Papers of Woodrow Wilson* (New York, 1925–1927, six vols.), II, 292, 455–56 (hereafter cited as *PPWW*).

7. LDB to Robert M. LaFollette, July 3, 1912, Brandeis MSS.

8. LDB to Norman Hapgood, July 3, 1912, *Ibid.*

9. *The New York Times,* August 29, 1912.

10. LDB to Alfred Brandeis, August 29, 1912, Brandeis MSS.

11. Link, *op. cit.,* I, 489.

12. John Wells Davidson, ed., *A Crossroads of Freedom: The 1912 Campaign Speeches of Woodrow Wilson* (New Haven, 1956), 79, 113, 171.

13. Wilson to LDB, September 27, 1912, Brandeis MSS.

14. "Suggestions for Letter of Governor Wilson on Trusts," enclosed in LDB to Wilson, September 30, 1912, in Woodrow Wilson Papers, Library of Congress.

15. Memorandum of conversations . . . , October 2–3, 1912, Brandeis MSS; LDB to Ray Stannard Baker, September 27, 1926, in the Ray Stannard Baker Papers, Library of Congress; Norman Hapgood to LDB, September 12, 1912, Brandeis MSS. Some of these articles appeared in LDB's collection entitled *Business—A Profession* (Boston, 1914).

16. Davidson, *op. cit.,* 393.

17. These quotes are all from "The Old Order Changeth," the first part of Woodrow Wilson, *The New Freedom*, edited by William E. Leuchtenburg (Englewood Cliffs, N.J., 1961), 25, 26.

18. Theodore Roosevelt, "The Trusts, the People, and the Square Deal," *The Outlook*, XCIX (November 18, 1911), 649.

19. Hofstadter, *The Age of Reform*, 248.

20. Louis Hartz, *The Liberal Tradition in America* (New York, 1955), 232. It has been argued that the bulk of concentration in industry had taken place prior to 1899, and that actually more, rather than less, competition was the rule by 1912. While statistically this may have been true, the perception of the progressive lagged behind this reality; the specter of monopoly did not really grow so frightening until 1906 or so. (See G. Warren Nutter, *The Extent of Enterprise Monopoly in the United States, 1899–1939* [Chicago, 1951], 144–47.)

21. *PPWW*, II, 410–11, 347.

22. Published as *Other People's Money, and How the Bankers Use It* (New York, 1914), it popularized many of the findings of the Pujo Committee.

23. Ray Stannard Baker, *Woodrow Wilson: Life and Letters* (Garden City, 1927–1939, eight vols.), III, 432; *PPWW*, III, 37.

24. Glass to Wilson, May 15, 1913, in Baker, *Wilson*, III, 151; William J. and Mary B. Bryan, *The Memoirs of William Jennings Bryan* (Philadelphia, 1925), 370; Joseph P. Tumulty, *Woodrow Wilson As I Know Him* (Garden City, 1921), 178–79.

25. Owen to Wilson, May 20, 1913, in Baker, *Wilson*, III, 161.

26. Alfred Lief, *Brandeis: The Personal History of an American Ideal* (New York, 1936), 205.

27. LDB to Wilson, June 14, 1913, Brandeis MSS.

28. By March 1, 1914, 7,571 banks had joined the system, while only 18 national banks remained aloof.

29. Belle Case and Fola LaFollette, *Robert M. LaFollette* (New York, 1953, two vols.), II, 486–87; see also "Legalizing the 'Money Power,'" *LaFollette's Weekly*, V (December 27, 1913), 1.

30. In October, LDB had thought the bill could be broadened, but had predicted that some of the defects would be corrected by antitrust legislation. (LDB to Samuel Untermyer, October 2, 1913, Brandeis MSS.)

31. David Houston, *Eight Years with Wilson's Cabinet* (Garden City, 1926, two vols.), I, 85–86; diary entry of January 16, 1914, in the Edward M. House Papers, Sterling Library, Yale University, New Haven, Conn.; J. J. Wilbur to Frank Trumbell, December 16, 1913, Vanderlip MSS; H. L. Higginson to Wilson, December 19, 1913, Wilson MSS.

32. Houston, *op. cit.*, I, 86; House Diary, October 28, 1913; LDB to Franklin K. Lane, December 12, 1913, Brandeis MSS.

33. *PPWW*, II, 348, 410–11, 455–56; Baker, *Wilson*, IV, 365–66.

34. House Committee on the Judiciary, *Hearings on Trust Legislation*, 62nd Cong., 2nd Sess. (Washington, 1912), 22; Senate Committee on Interstate Commerce, *Hearings . . . on Control of Corporations . . .*, 62nd Cong., 2nd Sess. (Washington, 1911), IV, 1291; Statement before Joint Committee of Massachusetts Legislature on Liquor Law, February 27, 1891, Brandeis MSS.

35. *Boston Globe*, March 9, 1905.

36. As late as July, 1914, Wilson still maintained that bigness per se did not bother him, but only "unrighteous methods" (Wilson to A. S. Burleson, July 27, 1914, cited in Diamond, *op. cit.*, 108). It would appear that the President never really understood the essence of the Brandeisian argument, although he had advocated it in 1912. LDB realized this later ("Notes of Interview of Louis D. Brandeis . . . ," Ray Stannard Baker MSS.).

37. Brandeis, "The Solution of the Trust Problem," *Harper's Weekly*, LVIII (November 8, 1913), 18–19.

38. *PPWW*, III, 81–88.

39. LDB to Alfred Brandeis, January 23, 1913, Brandeis MSS.

40. Untermyer to House, January 25, 1913, and House to Wilson, January 27, 1914, Wilson MSS.

41. William C. Adamson to LDB, January 29, 1914, Brandeis MSS; *Hearings . . . on Trust Legislation,* 63rd Cong., 2nd Sess. (Washington, 1914), Serial VII, Part 22.

42. LDB to James C. McReynolds, February 22, 1914, Brandeis MSS.

43. *Hearings . . . on Trust Legislation,* 63rd Cong., 2nd Sess., at 922; George Rublee to LDB, March 13, 1914, Brandeis MSS.

44. "Memorandum on LaFollette Bill," November 8, 1911, Brandeis MSS.

45. George Rublee, "The Original Plan and Early History of the Federal Trade Commission," *Proceedings of the Academy of Political Science,* XI (January, 1926), 115.

46. George Rublee Memoir, Oral History Research Office, Columbia University.

Chapter V

1. Like all movements involving great numbers of disparate groups and persons, Zionism is an extremely complex problem that does not lend itself easily to historical analysis. Every other sentence could, and perhaps should, be qualified in some way or another. There were Orthodox, Conservative, and Reform Jews, Sephardic and Askenazic, Eastern Europeans and Germans, not to mention all the adherents of numerous ideological schools that existed irregardless of religion. For the purpose of this chapter, I have attempted to differentiate only between the Eastern European Zionism of Weizmann and the American Reform Zionism of Brandeis. It should also be noted that there were a variety of elements in American progressivism. Although Brandeis represented a particular mode of that reform, I also ask the reader's indulgence in allowing me to generalize that his experience was reflective of the movement as a whole. I hope at a later time to expand this study into a larger form, where more attention may be paid to these subtleties.

2. *American Israelite,* June 3, 1897, and November 28, 1895, cited in Joseph P. Sternstein, "Reform Judaism and Zionism," *Herzl Year Book,* V (1963), 15.

3. However, some support for Zionism did exist among Reform Jews; see Herschel Levin, "The Other Side of the Coin," *ibid.,* 33–56.

4. Quoted in Samuel Halperin, *The Political World of American Zionism* (Detroit, 1961), 10.

5. Quoted in Eric F. Goldman, *Rendezvous with Destiny* (New York, 1960), 142.

6. Jacob Schiff to S. S. Wise, April 20, 1904, in Stephen S. Wise, *Challenging Years* (New York, 1949), 33.

7. Jacob deHaas, *Louis D. Brandeis: A Biographical Sketch* (New York, 1929), 8; John Higham, *Strangers in the Land* (New York, 1963), 26–27, 66–67.

8.   *The American Hebrew,* December 2, 1910; cf. Felix Frankfurter's views on religion in *Felix Frankfurter Reminisces* (New York, 1960), 290, 291.

9.   Solomon Schindler, *Messianic Expectations and Modern Judaism* (Boston, 1886), *passim;* Arthur Mann, *Yankee Reformers in an Urban Age* (New York, 1966), Ch. 3.

10.   Barbara M. Solomon, *Pioneers in Progress: The History of the Associated Jewish Philanthropies of Boston* (Boston, 1956), 52, 59, 176.

11.   LDB to A. E. Pinanski, March 12, 1909, Savings Bank Life Insurance Archives.

12.   This statement is based primarily on my work in editing LDB's letters, but is borne out by the testimony of one of his close associates. See Norman Hapgood, *The Changing Years* (New York, 1930), 197.

13.   Despite the repetition of this story in Wise, *op. cit.,* 185, and deHaas, *op. cit.,* 51, it has the ring of the apocryphal about it. From this writer's research, it seems doubtful that LDB would make such a statement, and then not follow it up at all for nearly fifteen years. This does not mean that I am in agreement with arguments that LDB became a Zionist for politically opportune reasons, but only that I question the truth of this story.

14.   Quoted in deHaas, *op. cit.,* 163.

15.   See "What Loyalty Demands," speech on 250th anniversary of the settlement of Jews in the United States, November 28, 1905, copy in Brandeis MSS; see also [Boston] *Jewish Advocate,* December 9, 1910.

16.   deHaas, *op. cit.,* 51–53; Wise, *op. cit.,* 185–86; Memorandum of LDB interview with Balfour, June 24, 1919, in Jacob deHaas Papers, American Zionist Archives, New York.

17.   Milton R. Konvitz, "Louis D. Brandeis," in Simon Noveck, ed., *Great Jewish Personalities in Modern Times* (New York, 1960), 295–316, at 300.

18.   deHaas, *Brandeis,* 54–55.

19.   Remarks accepting Provisional Committee chairmanship, August 30, 1914, in Solomon Goldman, ed., *Brandeis on Zionism* (Washington, 1942), 44: see also LDB to Bernard Richards, February 2, 1911, courtesy of Mr. Richards.

20.   deHaas, *Brandeis,* 163 (ca. 1914–1915).

21. Louis E. Levinthal, "Louis Dembitz Brandeis," *The American Jewish Yearbook 5703*, XLIV (1942), 45; see also Brandeis to Chaim Weizmann, January 13, 1918, in deHaas MSS.

22. Brandeis, "Address to Second Annual Conference on Palestine Land Development Council, May 27, 1923," *Brandeis on Zionism,* 130.

23. Ben-Gurion made the comment to LDB's granddaughter, who told me about it during an interview in July, 1969.

24. The most explicit statement is Yonathan Shapiro, "American Jews in Politics: The Case of Louis D. Brandeis," *American Jewish Historical Quarterly,* XV (1965), 199–211.

25. For Wilson's relation with LDB, see this book, Chapter 4, as well as Arthur S. Link, *Wilson* (Princeton, 1947–   , five volumes to date), I, 488–93; II, 10–15, 423–34; and IV, 323–27, 356–62.

26. See, for example, LDB to Morris Rotheberg, February 18, 1917, Brandeis MSS.

27. Ezekiel Rabinowitz, *Justice Louis D. Brandeis: The Zionist Chapter of His Life* (New York, 1968), 31.

28. deHaas, *Brandeis,* 68.

29. In 1916, LDB successfully challenged the leaders of the established lay organizations in calling for a democratically elected American Jewish Congress to replace the American Jewish Committee, which consisted of self-appointed members of different secular and charitable groups, and was headed by Cyrus Adler and Louis Marshall.

30. According to Stephen Wise, LDB's financial contributions were the greatest of any Zionist of his time. (Wise, *op. cit.,* 186.)

31. Boston *American,* July 3, 1915.

32. Max Isidor Bodenheimer, *Prelude to Israel* (New York and London, 1963), 11.

33. For Weizmann's early life, see his autobiography, *Trial and Error* (New York, 1949), Ch. 1–3. Weizmann's book is extremely personal and defensive, and should be used with care. See the criticisms compiled by Oskar K. Rabinowicz, *Fifty Years of Zionism: A Historical Analysis of Dr. Weizmann's "Trial and Error"* (London, 1952 ed.).

34. Norman Bentwich, "Chaim Weizmann," in Noveck, *op. cit.,* 270.

35. "The Jewish State and the Jewish Problem," in *Ten Essays on Zionism and Judaism,* trans. Leon Simon (London, 1922), 44.

36. Weizmann, *op. cit.,* 176.

37. See, for example, Achad Ha'am, "Summa Summarum" (1912), in *Ten Essays,* 132.

38. Wise, *op. cit.,* 26; Louis Lipsky, *A Gallery of Zionist Profiles* (New York, 1956), 56. Weizmann's autobiography is full of instances where he paints events in such terms, viz., "the messianic hope which we had read into the Balfour Declaration" (Weizmann, *op. cit.,* 218).

39. Frankfurter, *op. cit.,* 184–85.

40. It has been suggested that Weizmann cared for detail a great deal more than I allow, and that he had, in fact, been criticized for the plodding "one foot at a time" approach that he used in building up the colonies. I do not mean that Weizmann ignored details. He was, after all, a brilliant scientist, fully familiar with the scientific method. In his Zionist work, he could handle facts well when forced to, but he nearly always put off coming to grips with the facts until absolutely necessary. Then, because of poor planning, he had to work slowly, because he had failed to prepare money, people, or time in advance. An example of the difference between the two men in this regard can be seen in their proposals for dealing with malaria. After LDB returned from his 1919 trip to Palestine, he noted that large-scale colonization would be impossible until the malaria-breeding swamps were drained. Since colonization would be necessary to implement the Balfour Declaration, then the first step of the Zionist Organization ought to be swamp-draining. Weizmann, on the other hand, did not consider this realistic, and contended that the British would not provide money for such measures. Get people there, and work to make sure the British would keep their promises, he argued, instead of worrying about mosquitoes. It proved impossible, of course, to secure large-scale colonization until the necessary health and sanitation measures were taken.

41. Frankfurter, *op. cit.,* 178. LDB could be just as rigid and single-minded when he got onto something. In 1930, the American Zionists were trying to pressure the British government into a more flexible immigration policy for Palestine, and Harold Laski served as an informal mediary. In several letters to Holmes, Laski complained of LDB's failure to understand that compromise might be necessary, and that the British government was not about to act just because LDB said so, or even because it should. See Laski to Holmes, June 15, November 22 and 30, and December 27, 1930, in *Holmes–Laski Letters* (Cambridge, Mass., 1953), II, 1261, 1296, 1298–99, 1301–2.

42. Weizmann to LDB, September 19, 1917; LDB to Weizmann, September 24, 1917 (two cables); Weizmann to LDB, October 14, November 12, 1917, all in Brandeis MSS. See also Wise, *op. cit.*, 189.

43. LDB to Weizmann, January 13, 1918, DeHaas Papers.

44. deHaas, *Brandeis*, 96–97. The reader might infer a contradiction between LDB's faith in a capitalistic free-enterprise system (as explained in Chapter 3) and these comments. The answer lies in LDB's pragmatism. The United States was an advanced country which had grown utilizing an admittedly imperfect economic system; the seemingly inexhaustible natural resources had prevented a total despoilation of the common wealth by private businessmen. Palestine, on the other hand, was an undeveloped land, with very limited natural wealth. The circumstances were different, and different measures had to be adopted. What Brandeis sought was a balance between public and private sectors.

45. LDB to Jacob Billikopf, June 16, 1916, Brandeis MSS.

46. LDB to Alice Goldmark Brandeis, August 8, 1919, *Ibid.*

47. Bodenheimer, *op. cit.*, 292–93. LDB had made similar suggestions to Weizmann in 1919, but to no avail. Weizmann may have changed his mind in the intervening year because of LDB's increased stature among various world leaders, and his role in securing the mandate for Great Britain at the San Remo conference. It is interesting to speculate whether LDB's plan would have been accepted if he had been willing to take one of the seats on the triumvirate, perhaps giving another one to Weizmann. My own belief is that LDB's prestige, as well as his reputation for getting things done, might have tipped the balance in his favor.

48. Weizmann, *op. cit.*, 267; see also Maurice Samuel, *Level Sunlight* (New York, 1953), 30.

49. At one time, Herzl had been offered the territory of Uganda in which to establish a Jewish homeland. Although he favored any homeland over no homeland, the Eastern Europeans had soundly defeated him, charging that the only real homeland for the Jews must be Palestine.

50. See Arthur S. Link, "What Happened to the Progressive Movement in the 1920's?" *American Historical Review*, LXIV (1959), 833–51.

51. LDB also objected to Weizmann approving the use of land money to pay the expenses of some delegations from East and Central Europe to the London conference.

52. Lipsky, *op. cit.*, 56–57.

53. LDB to Julian Mack, June 21, 1921, Brandeis MSS.

54. *Protocols of the Twelfth Zionist Congress* (1921), 194, 288, quoted in Rabinowicz, *op. cit.,* 75–76.

55. Adolph Boehm, *Die Zionistische Bewegung* (Berlin, 1935–1937), II, 217, quoted in Rabinowicz, *op. cit.,* 75. LDB and his followers established a number of investment and donation funds which they ran independently of the world movement. The charges raised by some of Weizmann's followers that LDB was only interested in developing private enterprise in Palestine strike me as ridiculous. In speech after speech, in the Pittsburgh program and the *Zeeland* memorandum, he emphasized the need for cooperative enterprises and the maintenance by public agencies of all land, mineral, and utility rights. See Bentwich, "Weizmann," Noveck, *op. cit.,* 281; Lipsky, *op. cit.,* 57. They failed to understand that Brandeis wanted the agencies properly managed, as were the best of private businesses. As Frankfurter noted, "Brandeis wanted all the organs of the movement ... to be as conservatively competent as the National City Bank" (Frankfurter, *op. cit.,* 180).

56. Rabinowicz, *op. cit.,* 78.

57. S. M. Melamed, "L. D. Brandeis and Chaim Weizmann," *The Reflex,* II (May, 1928), 2.

Chapter VI

1. According to *The New York Times* (January 29, 1916), "Mr. Brandeis is essentially a contender, a striver after change and reforms. The Supreme Court by its very nature is the conservator of our institutions."

2. This generalization would have to be modified in certain cases, such as that of William Howard Taft. Despite his ineptness in the Ballinger controversy, Taft had a good record in such fields as antitrust prosecution and conservation. He opposed LDB not only because of the humiliation he had suffered in the Ballinger affair, but also because he had rather naïvely hoped that Wilson would appoint him to the Court, a dream that would finally be fulfilled by Warren Harding in 1921. Nevertheless, I believe that the overall lineup did reflect the clearest split that can be found between progressives and others. LDB himself wrote that "the fight that has come up shows clearly that my instinct that I could not afford to decline was correct. It would have been, in effect, deserting the progressive forces" (LDB to Alfred Brandeis, February 12, 1916, Brandeis MSS).

3. Amos Pinchot to LDB, June 6, 1916, Brandeis MSS.

4. LDB to Amos Pinchot, June 27, 1916, *Ibid.*

5. LDB also refused to discuss his colleagues. "Try as hard as I may," said Jacob Billikopf, "to get an expression of opinion regarding his colleagues, particularly Butler, McReynolds or Taft—no success." Cited in Alpheus T. Mason, *Brandeis: A Free Man's Life* (New York, 1946), 538.

6. LDB to Edward White, June 29, 1916; White to LDB, July 17, 1916; Brandeis MSS.

7. There is a collection of letters between LDB and Miss Grady in the Library of Brandeis University; there is a larger group, including correspondence with other officials, in the Archives of Savings Bank Life Insurance.

8. See Bernard Flexner, *Mr. Justice Brandeis and the University of Louisville* (Louisville, 1938).

9. Alpheus T. Mason, *William Howard Taft: Chief Justice* (New York, 1965), *passim.*

10. Wilson to Culberson, May 5, 1916, in United States Senate, *Hearings . . . on the Nomination of Louis D. Brandeis . . . ,* Senate Document 409, 64th Cong., 1st Sess. (Washington, 1916), II, 5–7.

11. LDB to Wilson, August 14, 1916, Brandeis MSS.

12. Stephen S. Wise, *Challenging Years* (New York, 1949), 179.

13. Mason, *Brandeis,* 525.

14. There are many references to meetings with LDB and to seeking advice from him scattered throughout the papers of various Wilson Administration figures.

15. This theme is explored in my *Big Steel and the Wilson Administration: A Study in Business-Government Relations* (Columbus, Ohio, 1969).

16. Theodore Roosevelt, *The Foes of Our Own Household* (New York, 1917), 122.

17. LDB to Edward M. House, January 9, 1918, Brandeis MSS.

18. LDB had failed to take into account personal animosities and jealousy. While Baker was undoubtedly overworked, he opposed the President's reorganization plan (which had been drawn along lines similar to LDB's suggestions) because he did not want Bernard Baruch to get the

job; he also wanted to maintain his own power and prerogatives. See Daniel Beaver, "Newton D. Baker and the Genesis of the War Industries Board, 1917–1918," *Journal of American History*, LII (1965), 43–58. Moreover, even after the inauguration of the administrative shakeup, petty jealousies and agency powers continued to prevent a clear delineation of responsibility. What both LDB and Wilson failed to take into account is that real power often resides at lower- and middle-management levels. Declaring that an agency head has certain powers does not lodge that power in the head; it must be transferred from other levels. See the revealing article by Robert D. Cuff, "Bernard Barauch: Symbol and Myth in Industrial Mobilization," *Business History Review*, XLIII (1969), 115–33.

19.   LDB to Alfred Brandeis, May 13, 1910, Brandeis MSS.

20.   The plank is printed in Mason, *Brandeis*, 519.

21.   LDB to Edward M. House, January 9, 1918, Brandeis MSS.

22.   LDB to Bainbridge Colby, June 14, 1921, in Bainbridge Colby Papers, Library of Congress; Colby to LDB, June 15, 1921, and Thomas L. Chadbourne to LDB, June 15, 1921, Brandeis MSS. Chadbourne, a prominent New York attorney, had many connections in the government and the Democratic party. Colby had been a Progressive Republican until 1916, when he rallied support for Wilson among the ex-Roosevelt backers. He was appointed to the U.S. Shipping Board, and in 1920 became Secretary of State. After Wilson left office, he and Colby opened a short-lived law practice.

23.   Enclosed in Wilson to LDB, June 20, 1921, Brandeis MSS.

24.   A copy of the "Document" is in the Colby MSS.

25.   Wilson to LDB, January 7, 1922; Wilson to Colby, April 11, 1922, Wilson MSS.

26.   See Andrew Sinclair, *The Available Man: Warren Gameliel Harding* (New York, 1965), Ch. 10.

27.   "The Living Law," 10 *Illinois Law Review* 461 (1916).

28.   Chief Justice Harlan Fiske Stone told Mason that LDB "was strongly of the belief that a Justice of the Court should devote himself singlemindedly to his activities as a Justice, without undertaking to engage in any outside activities."

29.   See William E. Leuchtenburg, "The New Deal and the Analogue of War," in John Braeman *et al.*, eds., *Change and Continuity in Twentieth-Century America* (Columbus, 1964), 81–144.

30. Thomas G. Corcoran and Benjamin V. Cohen to Felix Frankfurter, June 18, 1934, in Freedman, *Roosevelt & Frankfurter*, 223–25; LDB to Elizabeth Brandeis Raushenbush, June 8, 1934, courtesy of Mrs. Raushenbush; Raul A. Raushenbush, "Starting Unemployment Compensation in Wisconsin," *Unemployment Insurance Review* (April–May, 1967), 17–24.

31. Interview with Miss Mary Switzer, head of the Division of Rehabilitation of the Department of Health, Education and Welfare, Summer, 1967.

32. An excellent study of the ideological and administrative problems of the neo-Brandeisians can be found in Ellis Wayne Hawley, *The New Deal and the Problem of Monopoly: A Study in Economic Ambivalence* (Princeton, 1966).

33. J. Willard Hurst, "Who is the 'Great' Appellate Judge?" 24 *Indiana Law Journal* 394, 398 (1949).

34. Felix Frankfurter, "Mr. Justice Brandeis and the Constitution," 45 *Harvard Law Review* 33, 104 (1931).

35. *New York Central Railroad Company v. Winfield*, 244 U.S. 147, 154 (1917).

36. In Felix Frankfurter, ed., *Mr. Justice Brandeis* (New Haven, 1932), 3.

37. Walter Raushenbush, *Brandeis as Jurist: Craftsmanship with Inspiration* (Louisville, 1965).

38. Harold J. Laski, "Mr. Justice Brandeis," *Harper's Magazine,* CLXVIII (January, 1934), 211.

39. 262 U.S. 276, 289 (1922); the statement, by Allyn F. Young, is cited in Frankfurter, "Mr. Justice Brandeis and the Constitution," 60.

40. For instance, *Munn v. Illinois,* 94 U.S. 113 (1876).

41. 169 U.S. 466 (1898).

42. See also his dissent in *St. Louis and O'Fallon Ry. Company v. United States,* 279 U.S. 461, 488 (1929).

43. Holmes once wrote, "We are sitting and having cases that I dislike about rates and the Interstate Commerce Commission. I listen with respect but without envy to questions by Brandeis and Butler using the words of railroading and rate-making that I imperfectly understand. To be familiar with business is a great (secondary) advantage. Someone said of Brandeis, He is not afraid of a Balance-Sheet. His experience at the

bar is an infinite advantage in many cases." (Holmes to Harold J. Laski, February 22, 1929, in Mark A. DeWolfe Howe, ed., *The Holmes–Laski Letters* [Cambridge, 1953], II, 1135.)

44. *Quaker State Cab Company v. Pennsylvania,* 277 U.S. 389 (1928).

45. *Ibid.,* at 410–11.

46. 288 U.S. 517 (1933).

47. *Ibid.,* 541, at 574.

48. Samuel J. Konefsky, *The Legacy of Holmes and Brandeis* (New York, 1956), 156–57.

49. 288 U.S. 580.

50. *The Common Law* (Boston, 1881), 1.

51. Judge Jerome Frank once noted that "much harm is done by the myth that, merely by putting on a black robe and taking the oath of office as judge, a man ceases to be human and strips himself of all predilections, and becomes a passionless thinking machine." Brandeis's great personal charm and warmth were normally hidden from outsiders by his aloofness and deeply felt sense of privacy. His letters, with rare exceptions, were rather formal, and as an editor of the *Brandeis Letters,* I can testify to Paul Freund's observation that many of LDB's personal communications read like the text of a Brandeis brief. "Mr. Justice Brandeis: A Centennial Memoir," 70 *Harvard Law Review* 769, 773 (1957).

52. *American Column and Lumber Company v. United States,* 257 U.S. 377 (1921).

53. *Ibid.,* 410–1.

54. *Ibid.,* 412, at 418–9.

55. Frankfurter, "Mr. Justice Brandeis and the Constitution," 79.

56. *DiSanto v. Pennsylvania,* 273 U.S., 34, 42 (1927); see also his concurring opinion in *Ashwander v. Tennessee Valley Authority,* 297 U.S., 288, 341 (1936).

57. Paul Freund, *On Understanding the Supreme Court* (Boston, 1950), 67. The cases referred to were: *Bradley Electric Light Company v. Clapper,* 284 U.S. 221 (1931); *John Hancock Mutual Life Insurance Company v. Yates,* 299 U.S. 178 (1936); *Yarborough v. Yarborough,* 290 U.S. 202 (1933).

58. *New State Ice Company v. Liebman,* 285 U.S. 262, 279 (1932).

59. *Ibid.,* 280, at 311.

60. *Ibid.*

61. See Konefsky, *op. cit.,* Chs. 9, 10.

62. *Truax v. Corrigan,* 257 U.S. 312, 354, at 376 (1921).

63. *Abrams v. United States,* 250 U.S. 616 (1919).

64. *Schaefer v. United States,* 251 U.S. 466, 482, at 495 (1920).

65. *Pierce v. United States,* 252 U.S. 239, 253, at 273 (1920).

66. 274 U.S. 357, 372 (1927). Miss Whitney was the niece of Mr. Justice Field.

67. *Ibid.,* at 376–79.

68. Alpheus T. Mason, *Supreme Court from Taft to Warren* (Baton Rouge, La., 1958), 31.

69. *Adkins v. Children's Hospital,* 261 U.S. 525, 559–60 (1923). LDB disqualified himself in this case because his daughter Elizabeth was Secretary to the District's Minimum Wage Board. He would undoubtedly have joined in Holmes's dissent otherwise. The massive brief filed by Frankfurter ran over 1,100 pages, and like LDB's earlier brief, was published by the National Consumers' League.

70. See his dissents in *Truax v. Corrigan; Burns Baking Co. v. Bryan,* 264 U.S. 504, 517 (1924); and *Quaker City Cab Co. v. Pennsylvania.*

71. Laski to Holmes, January 13, 1918, in *Holmes–Laski Letters,* I, 127; see also Holmes to Laski, November 5, 1923, and November 21, 1924, in *ibid.,* 556, 675.

72. Holmes to Laski, December 27, 1925, *ibid.,* 810.

73. Holmes to Laski, June 16, 1919, *ibid.,* 212.

74. Holmes to Laski, June 11, 1920, *ibid.,* 268. Brandeis, however, continued to twit Holmes about his simplistic economic views.

75. Eric Goldman, *Rendezvous with Destiny* (New York, 1956), 105,

76. LDB to Woodrow Wilson, April 15, 1923, Brandeis MSS.

77. Dean Acheson, "Mr. Justice Brandeis," 55 *Harvard Law Review* 191, 192 (1941).

Chapter VII

1. Quoted in Felix Frankfurter, "Mr. Justice Brandeis and the Constitution," 45 *Harvard Law Review* 33 (1931).

2. Henry D. Swift to LDB, October 9, 1890; LDB to Alfred Brandeis, February 7, 1912; Brandeis MSS.

3. LDB to Alfred Brandeis, May 1, 1910, *Ibid*.

4. Conversation with Alfred Lief, May 19, 1934, in Lief, *The Brandeis Guide to the Modern World* (Boston, 1941), 211.

5. Paul Freund, "Mr. Justice Brandeis," in Allison Dunham and Philip B. Kurland, eds., *Mr. Justice* (Chicago, 1956), 118; see also LDB to Alice Goldmark, October 27, 1890.

6. LDB to Alice Goldmark, December 9, 1890, courtesy of Mrs. Raushenbush.

7. LDB to Alfred Brandeis, January 16, 1927, Brandeis MSS.

8. Cited in George Mowry, *Theodore Roosevelt and the Progressive Movement* (Madison, 1946), 212.

9. Memorandum, April 14, 1903, in Lief, *op. cit.*, 38.

10. Various sources, all in *ibid.*, 209.

11. Quoted in Daniel Aaron, *Men of Good Hope: A Story of American Progressives* (New York, 1951), xii.

12. LDB to Robert W. Bruere, February 25, 1922, Brandeis MSS.

13. LDB to Edwin Doak Mead, November 9, 1895, in Henry D. Lloyd Papers, The State Historical Society, Madison, Wisconsin.

14. LDB to Edwin Bacon, August 6, 1890, Brandeis MSS.

15. "Wage-Earners' Life Insurance," *Collier's Weekly*, XXXVII (September 15, 1906), 16 *ff*.

16. "If we should get tomorrow the necessary legislation without having achieved that process of education, we could not make a practical working success of the plan" (Brandeis to Henry Morgenthau, November 20, 1906). The best available study is Alpheus T. Mason, *The Brandeis Way* (Princeton, 1938).

17. Paul Freund, *On Understanding the Supreme Court* (Boston, 1950), 74.

18. Oliver Wendell Holmes to Louis Einstein, May 22, 1919, in James Bishop Peabody, ed., *The Holmes–Einstein Letters* (New York, 1964), 187.

19. Harold J. Laski to Oliver Wendell Holmes, December 14, 1924, August 12, 1933, in Mark DeWolfe Howe, ed., *Holmes–Laski Letters* (Cambridge, 1953), I, 687, II, 1448; see also Laski, "Mr. Justice Brandeis," *Harper's Magazine*, CLXVIII (January, 1934), 209–18.

20. Frankfurter to Arthur M. Schlesinger, Jr., June 18, 1963, in Max Freedman, ed., *Roosevelt & Frankfurter: Their Correspondence, 1928–1945* (Boston, 1967), 26.

21. Freund, "Mr. Justice Brandeis," 104.

22. Freund, *On Understanding the Supreme Court*, 49.

23. LDB to Alfred Brandeis, May 27, 1906, *Ibid.*

24. LDB to Edmund Billings, December 16, 1903, *Ibid.*

25. LDB to Warren A. Reed, September 3, 1907, *Ibid.*

26. Edward Adler to LDB, March 20, 1903, *Ibid.*

27. Interview with Elizabeth Brandeis Raushenbush, July 17, 1969.

28. LDB to Alice Goldmark, February 26, 1891, courtesy of Mrs. Raushenbush.

29. See, for example, LDB to E. A. Filene, June 1, 1901, and to Curtis Guild, March [?], 1906, Brandeis MSS.

30. Max Lerner, *Ideas Are Weapons: The History and Uses of Ideas* (New York, 1939), 76.

31. There is a file of letters between LDB and his former secretary, Alice H. Grady, who became head of the savings bank program. This file, stretching over many years after he had gone on the Court, is in the basement of the Brandeis University Library.

32.   Lerner, *op. cit.*, 83.

33.   See, among others, Samuel P. Hays, *The Response to Industrialism, 1885–1914* (Chicago, 1957); Robert Wiebe, *The Search for Order, 1877–1920* (New York, 1967); Richard Hofstadter, *The Age of Reform: From Bryan to F.D.R.* (New York, 1955); Samuel P. Hays, "The Politics of Reform in Municipal Government in the Progressive Era," *Pacific Northwest Quarterly*, LV (1964), 157–69.

34.   Lawrence A. Cremin, *The Transformation of the School* (New York, 1961), Part One, *passim.*

35.   The eulogy is reprinted as "Mr. Justice Brandeis," 55 *Harvard Law Review* 191 (1941).

BIBLIOGRAPHY

Nearly all of the ideas dealt with in these essays have grown out of work connected with editing the *Letters of Louis D. Brandeis* (Albany, N.Y., 1971—). For this, the prime source was the Papers of Louis Dembitz Brandeis located at the University of Louisville Law Library; supplementing this large collection were dozens of repositories containing the papers of numerous progressive and Zionist leaders.

Brandeis's writings are available in several places. His early articles are reprinted in *Business—A Profession* (Boston, 1914), while his exposé of the money trust, originally serialized in *Harper's Weekly*, was published as *Other People's Money, and How the Bankers Use It* (New York, 1914). Both books were reprinted in inexpensive editions during the 1930's, and a recent edition of *Other People's Money* (1967) carried a fine introductory essay by Richard M. Abrams. Two collections gathered by Alfred Lief provide superficial gleanings of LDB's opinions on a variety of subjects: *The Social and Economic Views of Mr. Justice Brandeis* (New York, 1930) and *The Brandeis Guide to the Modern World* (Boston, 1941). The best sampling of LDB's work is undoubtedly *The Curse of Bigness*, edited by Osmond K. Fraenkel (New York, 1934). Zionist writings are to be found in Solomon Goldman, ed., *Brandeis on Zionism* (Washington, 1942). A good guide to the corpus of Brandeisian literature is Roy M. Mersky, *Louis Dembitz Brandeis, 1856–1941, A Bibliography* (New Haven, 1958).

The best single source for LDB's life is Alpheus Thomas Mason, *Brandeis: A Free Man's Life* (New York, 1946). Mason has written a number of subsidiary studies on different facets of LDB's career: *Brandeis: Lawyer and Judge in the Modern State* (Princeton, 1933); *The Brandeis Way* (Princeton, 1938), dealing with Savings Bank Life Insurance; *Bureaucracy Convicts Itself* (New York, 1941), about the Pinchot-Ballinger affair; and, with Henry Lee Staples, *The Fall of a Railroad Empire: Brandeis and the New Haven Merger Battle* (Syracuse, N.Y., 1947). Useful

202   A MIND OF ONE PIECE

corrections to the last two are James L. Penick, Jr. *Progressive Politics and Conservation: The Ballinger-Pinchot Affair* (Chicago, 1968), and Richard M. Abrams, "Brandeis and the New Haven—Boston & Maine Merger Battle Revisited," *Business History Review*, XXXVI (1962), 408–30. Material on the garment workers Protocol can be found in Louis Levine, *The Women's Garment Workers* (New York, 1924) and Joel Seidman, *The Needle Traders* (New York, 1942), as well as in numerous contemporary articles. Because of his involvement as arbitrator, LDB wrote relatively little himself on the Protocol, although he was extremely proud of it.

The overall view of progressive reform is drawn from several sources, of which the following works have been most useful: Robert Wiebe, *The Search for Order, 1870–1920* (New York, 1967); Samuel P. Hays, *The Response to Industrialism, 1885–1914* (Chicago, 1957); Richard Hofstadter, *The Age of Reform: From Bryan to F.D.R.* (New York, 1955); and Eric F. Goldman, *Rendezvous with Destiny* (New York, 1960). Also invaluable have been three volumes in the New American Nation series: George E. Mowry, *The Era of Theodore Roosevelt and the Birth of Modern America, 1900–1912* (New York, 1958); Arthur S. Link, *Woodrow Wilson and the Progressive Era, 1910–1917* (New York, 1954); and William E. Leuchtenburg, *Franklin D. Roosevelt and the New Deal, 1932–1940* (New York, 1963). For the 1920's, see Leuchtenburg's *The Perils of Prosperity, 1914–1932* (Chicago, 1958).

For the Boston years, I have relied heavily on Arthur Mann, *Yankee Reformers in the Urban Age* (New York, 1966) and Richard M. Abrams, *Conservatism in a Progressive Era* (Cambridge, Mass., 1964). There are numerous studies of the Brahmins, of which the most useful were Frederic C. Jaher, "Aristocracy in America: The Case of the Boston Brahmins," in *The Age of Industrialism* (New York, 1968), and Barbara M. Solomon, *Ancestors and Immigrants: A Changing New England Tradition* (Cambridge, Mass., 1956). George Wilson Pierson has written an excellent study of the difficulties in trying to come to grips with the area in "The Obstinate Concept of New England: A Study in Denudation," *New England Quarterly*, XXVIII (1955), 3–17. Library shelves are filled with biographies and autobiographies of leading Bostonians. The elder Mark Howe seemingly chronicled every important and semi-important Brahmin of the latter nineteenth century. Better than any of them, however, is the marvelous *Education of Henry Adams* (Boston, 1918), which is *sui generis*. The older literary tradition can be looked at in Van Wyck Brooks, *The Flowering of New England* (New York, 1936). Changing views on immigrants are described in John Higham, *Strangers in the Land* (New Brunswick, N.J., 1963).

For the background of the *Muller* case, see especially Arnold M. Paul, *Conservative Crisis and the Rule of Law: Attitudes of Bar and Bench, 1887–1895* (Ithaca, 1960) and the more comprehensive James Willard Hurst, *The Growth of American Law: The Law Makers* (Boston, 1950). A central figure in the drive for legal reform was Oliver Wendell Holmes, Jr., and he has been well-served by his biographer, Mark DeWolfe Howe, in *Justice Oliver Wendell Holmes: The Shaping Years,*

1841–1870 (Cambridge, Mass., 1957) and *The Proving Years, 1870–1882* (1963). See also Holmes, *The Common Law* in the John Harvard edition with introduction by Howe (Cambridge, Mass., 1963) and *Collected Legal Papers* (New York, 1920). A brief yet incisive exegesis which places Holmes in a broad intellectual and historical context is Morton White, *Social Thought in America: The Revolt against Formalism* (Boston, 1957). Conservative thought can be traced in Robert G. McCloskey, *American Conservatism in the Age of Enterprise, 1865–1910* (New York, 1964) and Sidney Fine, *Laissez-Faire and the General Welfare State* (Ann Arbor, Mich., 1956). A useful revisionist article about Thomas McIntyre Cooley is Alan Jones, "Thomas M. Cooley and 'Laissez-Faire Constitutionalism': A Reconsideration," *Journal of American History*, LIII (1967), 751–71.

Brandeis's law practice is revealed in his letters, but the best single account is the memoir by his law partner, Edward F. McClennen, "Louis D. Brandeis as a Lawyer," 33 *Massachusetts Law Quarterly* I (1948). David W. Levy provides a broad perspective in "The Lawyer as Judge: Brandeis' View of the Legal Profession," 22 *Oklahoma Law Review* 374 (1969). The two most important statements by LDB himself are "The Opportunity in the Law," 39 *American Law Review* 555 (1905), reprinted in *Business—A Profession*, and "The Living Law," 10 *Illinois Law Review* 461 (1916), reprinted in *The Curse of Bigness*. The brief in the *Muller* case is in *Women in Industry...* (New York, 1908); other briefs in welfare cases are summarized in Josephine C. Goldmark, *Fatigue and Efficiency* (New York, 1912), and "The Constitution and the Minimum Wage," *The Survey*, XXXIII (February 6, 1915), 490–94, 521–24. Background on the *Muller* brief is ch. 13 of Josephine C. Goldmark, *Impatient Crusader: Florence Kelley's Life Story* (Urbana, Ill., 1953).

Changing economic conditions are documented and examined in scores of books. Statistics may be found in G. Warren Nutter, *The Extent of Enterprise Monopoly in the United States, 1899–1939* (Chicago, 1951); more lurid exposes are Henry Demarest Lloyd, *Wealth Against Commonwealth* (New York, 1894), which greatly impressed Brandeis, and Matthew Josephson, *The Robber Barons* (New York, 1934). A balanced overview is John A. Garraty, *The New Commonwealth, 1877–1890* (New York, 1968).

Business thought can be found in Arthur Jerome Eddy, *The New Competition* (Chicago, 1916, 5th ed.); Charles R. VanHise, *Concentration and Control* (New York, 1912); and Edward N. Hurley, *The Awakening of Business* (Garden City, 1917). The classic political statement of these ideas is Herbert Croly, *The Promise of American Life* (New York, 1909). In addition to Fine and McCloskey (cited above), see Edward C. Kirkland, *Dream and Thought in the Business Community, 1860–1900* (Ithaca, 1956) and Irvin C. Wyllie, *The Self-Made Man in America* (New Brunswick, N.J., 1954).

Brandeis's attack on monopolies is found in many places, most notably in his muckraking articles and testimony before various congressional committees; a full listing is in Mersky's bibliography, pp. 14–27. The most interesting exposition of the supposed futility of the Brandeisian approach is Gabriel Kolko, *The Triumph of Conservatism* (New York, 1963). Alfred D. Chandler first set forth the thesis concerning the connection between urbanism and industrialism in "The Beginnings of 'Big Business' in American Industry," *Business History Review*, XXXIII (1959), 1–31. Modern economic theory concerning industrial size and monopoly is in John Kenneth Galbraith, *American Capitalism* (Boston, 1956) and *The New Industrial State* (Boston, 1969). Oligopolistic behavior is examined in J. M. Clark, "Toward a Concept of Workable Competition," *American Economic Review*, XXX (1940), 241–56, and Edward H. Chamberlain, *The Theory of Monopolistic Competition* (Cambridge, Mass., 1956, 7th ed.)

Woodrow Wilson's papers and speeches have been gathered together by Ray Stannard Baker and William E. Dodd, *The Public Papers of Woodrow Wilson* (New York, 1925–1927, six vols.), but that is being supplanted by the definitive *Papers of Woodrow Wilson*, edited by Arthur S. Link and his associates in an edition that will ultimately run forty volumes (Princeton, 1966—). Similarly, the authorized biography by Baker, *Woodrow Wilson: Life and Letters* (Garden City, 1927–1939, eight vols.) is now outdated by Link's *Wilson* (Princeton, 1947—, five vols. to date). The complete 1912 speeches are collected in John Wells Davidson, ed., *A Crossroads of Freedom* (New Haven 1956), while a more popular version was *The New Freedom* (Garden City, 1913). The best bibliographic essay on the years 1910 to 1917 is in the paperback edition of Link, *Woodrow Wilson and the Progressive Era* (New York, 1963). Many of the sources cited there support the general contention that Brandeis was an influential figure in the Wilson administration, but none attempt to analyze the source of that influence. Urofsky, *Big Steel and the Wilson Administration* (Columbus, 1969), attempts to connect political and economic trends.

There is no good book covering American Zionism. The early years are treated carefully in Marnin Feinstein, *American Zionism, 1884–1904* (New York, 1965), while Samuel Halperin, *The Political World of American Zionism* (Detroit, 1961) examines American influence in the founding of the state of Israel. Brandeis's role is treated in a near-idolatrous manner by Jacob deHaas in *Louis D. Brandeis: A Biographical Sketch* (New York, 1929). The anti-Brandeisian attitude is exemplified by Louis Lipsky's chapter on Brandeis in *A Gallery of Zionist Profiles* (New York, 1956). Chaim Weizmann's opinion of Brandeis can be found in various places in his autobiography, *Trial and Error* (New York, 1949), but the book must be used with great care and has a number of factual errors. Other facets of the Brandeis-Weizmann controversy appear in the numerous autobiographies which the prolific Zionists ground out. The best are probably Stephen S. Wise, *Challenging Years* (New York, 1949 and *Felix Frankfurter Reminisces* (New York, 1960), but all of them have a unique character as varied as the Zionist movement itself. Also useful are the many annual indexes and yearbooks put out by various Jewish organizations. The charges of political opportunism are leveled by Yonathan Shapiro in "American Jews in Politics: The Case of Louis D. Brandeis," *American Jewish Historical Quarterly*, XV (1965), 199–211.

The fight over the nomination of Brandeis to the Supreme Court is best handled by Mason in *Brandeis: A Free Man's Life*, chapters 30 and 31, but see also Alden Todd, *Justice on Trial* (New York, 1964). Brandeis's involvement with the Wilson administration while on the bench has been gleaned primarily from manuscript sources, as well as some memoirs. His continued work for Zionism, Savings Bank Life Insurance, and the University of Louisville were not kept secret. There is no published material on the Document; and the story has been pieced together from evidence in the Brandeis, Wilson, and Colby Papers.

During the New Deal Brandeis again played a shadowy role, one that is still not spotlighted by much published material. Ellis Wayne Hawley, *The New Deal and the Problem of Monopoly: A Study in Economic Ambivalence* (Princeton, 1966) accurately portrays the vicissitudes of the Brandeisian philosophy during the Roosevelt years, as well as the intellectual influence exercised by the Justice. The letters between Felix Frankfurter and Franklin Roosevelt, edited by Max Freedman in *Roosevelt & Frankfurter: Their Correspondence, 1928–1945* (Boston, 1967), indicates some of Brandeis's influence. In the Roosevelt Papers at Hyde Park is an extensive correspondence between the President and Norman Hapgood, in which the journalist conveyed the jurist's suggestions to the politician. Interviews with New Deal figures, such as Mary Swizer and Paul Raushenbush, and examination of manuscript collections have confirmed the extent of Brandeis's participation in policy matters.

The literature on Brandeis as jurist is overwhelming, and it is difficult to determine where to start. There is, of course, the extensive corpus of Brandeisian opinions, both in the majority and in dissent, to be found in *United Stated Reports* from 1917 to 1939. Moreover, Alexander M. Bickel, *The Unpublished Opinions of Mr. Justice Brandeis* (Cambridge, Mass., 1957), provides a masterful insight into the research LDB did that never saw its way into print. For Holmes and Brandeis, a useful work is Samuel J. Konefsky, *The Legacy of Holmes and Brandeis* (New York, 1956). Felix Frankfurter wrote extensively on Brandeis; see especially his "Mr. Justice Brandeis and the Constitution," 45 *Harvard Law Review* 33 (1931) and *Mr. Justice Brandeis* (New Haven, 1932), which he edited. Brandeis's former law clerks have also written at length about him. See, for example, Paul A. Freund, "Mr. Justice Brandeis: A Centennial Memoir," 70 *Harvard Law Review* 769 (1956), and "Mr. Justice Brandeis," in Allison Dunham and Philip B. Kurkland, eds., *Mr. Justice* (Chicago, 1956); see also Freund's *On Understanding the Supreme Court* (Boston, 1950). J. Willard Hurst has dealt with Brandeis in *The Growth of American Law* (Boston, 1950) and "Who is the 'Great' Appellate Judge?" 24 *Indiana Law Journal* 394 (1949). An extremely appreciative analysis is Harold J. Laski, "Mr. Justice Brandeis," *Harper's Magazine*, CLXVIII (January, 1934), 209–218. For additional citation, see the Mersky pamphlet, pp. 31–44.

INDEX